The Meaning of Socialism

The Meaning of Socialism

Michael Luntley

Open ✲ Court
La Salle, Illinois

For Max

OPEN COURT and the above logo are registered in the
U.S. Patent and Trademark Office.

Published by arrangement with
Gerald Duckworth & Co. Ltd., London.

First printing 1990

Library of Congress Cataloging-in-Publication Data

Luntley, Michael, 1953–
   The meaning of socialism/Michael Luntley.
     p. cm.
   Includes bibliographical references and index.
   ISBN 0-8126-9113-X (cloth).—ISBN 0-8126-9114-8 (pbk.)
   1. Socialism. I. Title.
HX73.L87   1989   90-41124
335—dc20   CIP

Contents

Introduction

1. Markets, Values and Traditions

2. Ownership, Capital and the Economy

Contents

3. Criticising Traditions:
solving *the* problem in social theory

4. Freedom and Choice

5. Justice, Equality and Citizenship

6. Democracy and the Rule of Law

7. The Lion and the Unicorn: the peculiarities of English socialism

To allow the market mechanism to be sole director of the fate of human beings and their natural environment ... would result in the demolition of society ... Robbed of the protective covering of cultural institutions, human beings would perish from the effects of social exposure; they would die as the victims of acute social dislocation through vice, perversion, crime and starvation. Nature would be reduced to its elements, neighbourhoods and landscapes defiled, rivers polluted, military safety jeopardized, the power to produce food and raw materials destroyed. Finally, the market administration of purchasing power would periodically liquidate business enterprise, for shortages and surfeits of money would prove as disastrous to business as floods and droughts in primitive society ... no society could stand the effects of such a system ... unless its human and natural substance as well as its business organization was protected against the ravages of this satanic mill.

Karl Polanyi, *Origins of our Time:*
The Great Transformation (London 1945)

FOREWORD
TO THE AMERICAN EDITION
Henry Rosemont, Jr.

If asked our views about what constituted the American
Dream, I suspect strongly that a great many of us would say
something like the following: 'a reasonable level of material
well-being for all, with additional material goods for those who,
by dint of ability and effort, fairly earn them; the freedom to
pursue one's own projects and interests so long as they do not
infringe on the similar freedom of others; to have the opportunity to belong to a group, or groups, and to be bound together
with all other Americans by a willingness to make sacrifices to
spread and preserve this way of life against those who would
subvert it.'

Whatever the merits of this characterization may have been
in the past, it is not a possible vision for us to carry forward un-
changed into the twenty-first century. A number of ideas and
events have come together in recent years to make it impera-
tive for all citizens of the United States to begin rethinking
fundamental questions about the worth and significance of
their lives individually and collectively.

The ongoing weakening of Stalinist forms of government in
Eastern Europe and the Soviet Union is rendering ever more
obsolete the ideology of anti-communism which has domi-
nated — and enervated — much American thinking throughout
the Twentieth Century. Always more spectral than real, the
'Red Menace' now exists only in the minds of a very few true be-
lievers, making it difficult any longer to define our American-
ness in terms of struggling against it. The lifting of the dead
weight of anti-communist ideology from our thinking is probably the most liberating conceptual revolution that Americans
of the last three generations have experienced. Now we can
think new (or very old and venerable) thoughts; now we can
contemplate truly promoting the good, rather than merely
mitigating (real or imagined) evil.

For many people, the obverse of anti-communism has been

pro-capitalism, but this dimension of U. S. ideology, too, can no longer be credited. A long-held American belief has been that the best way to eliminate poverty is not to redistribute wealth, but to increase productivity; by increasing the size of the economic pie, the have-nots would get a larger share, without unjustly taking from those who had 'earned' more. The history of the United States shows clearly that this has not happened, yet repeated failures have always been met with calls for ever more productivity (and perhaps a bit of social tinkering), which is not surprising, even when the facts indicate otherwise; all of us would like to believe that the disadvantaged can be aided without disadvantaging others in any way. But we can no longer think in this way, because what we have learned from the environmental sciences, and about which there is no longer any doubt, is that the size of the possible pie is decidedly finite, and its upper limit has just about been reached, a few expressions of blind faith in star-wars technology notwithstanding. Without considering issues of the fair redistribution of wealth, then, the only response to continued and growing poverty in the U. S. must be callous indifference.

Still another facet of the American Dream has been called into question by the very success of industrial capitalism in this country. A significant number of American homes now have telephones and television sets in almost every room; two or three bathrooms, an equal number of cars in the driveway; microwave ovens, swimming pools, VCRs, and much more. Yet a sense of aimlessness and helplessness is growing in these homes no less than among the homeless. All of the world's philosophical and religious traditions have been in agreement that material things can never be constitutive of the good life, but it appears to be the sheer productivity of our industrial juggernaut that is bringing home the truth of 'not by bread alone'.

The convergence of these and other ideas and events are making it painfully evident that significant parts of the American Dream are just that: dreams. To believe that increased productivity will end poverty is a naive dream; to believe that ownership and consumption of that productivity can bring human happiness and contentment is a barren dream; and to believe that in the cause of productivity, our purple mountains and plains can continue to be despoiled without losing their majesty and fruit, is an impossible dream.

To be sure, it was better to have had these dreams than the nightmares of Stalin's purge trials, Pol Pot's Kampuchea, or Ceausescu's Romania. But the collapse of these dictatorial regimes cannot make us complacent, because we cannot address the future by looking only to the side, or backward. It may be well and good to celebrate how far we have come, and we have arguably done better than many others; any celebration must be brief, however, for we must face squarely the fact that we still have a very long way to go, and the ecological clock is ticking away. We are now in need of a different American Dream, and must struggle to develop and sophisticate a fresh conception of the good life.

And we must develop this conception collectively, as citizens, not as individuals. To insist upon this point is the basis on which Michael Luntley has admirably begun rebuilding the conceptual foundations of progressive political thought. Americans have long been wary of ideas that 'smacked of socialism', but the increasingly obvious moral bankruptcy of both communist (party) and capitalist ways of thinking require that we overcome our wariness, especially if socialist principles can be seen to be reflective of many of our basic moral convictions.

At first glance *The Meaning of Socialism* will probably strike most readers as odd and/or troublesome. Many socialists will probably be put off at first reading by Luntley's refusal to base his socialism on the necessity of public ownership of the means of production, and his insistence that small businesses are more compatible with socialist than with capitalist forms of social and economic organization. Liberals will be troubled by his cogent attacks on entitlement theories, conservatives surprised by his advocacy of communities and the importance of traditions. And probably everyone will be taken aback initially by the fact that Luntley does not ground his socialism in any of the concepts on which political theories are usually grounded: democracy, freedom, justice, or equality.

Rather does he ground socialism in the belief that there is such a thing as the good life, and that such a life is good independently of our thinking that it is. A basic tenet of Western political theory since the time of Hobbes, central to the En-

lightenment ideal, and enshrined in the American Dream, has
been the claim that the good cannot be ascertained for all, from
which it follows that the primary function of governments must
be to create and maintain institutions which will allow each
autonomous individual to pursue his or her own freely-chosen
definition of the good. In this sense, modern Western political
philosophy, and moral philosophy as well, have been value-
free, in that they emphasize procedure and are empty of substantive content. If, for example, you wonder whether you
should pursue a career in scholarship or politics; what it is to be
a friend; how to raise a family; if you wonder about any of these
or numerous other questions about the good, the books of modern Western moral and political philosophers are silent, for
they can have nothing to say that is not formal and procedural,
and such questions are substantive, hence must belong to the
private and not the public realm.

From such considerations it must follow that peoples' preferences solely determine what is preferred; their desires define
what is desirable. In sharp contrast, Michael Luntley posits the
Good Principle: "there is more to the achievement of the good
life than the satisfaction of individuals' actual preferences"
(p. 11). To accept this principle is to acknowledge the authority
of the good, and deference to that authority is whereby our lives
have worth and signficance. *The Meaning of Socialism* is not itself an account of the good life. Rather does it sketch out the
kind of society in which many and varied accounts of the good
life can be put forward for consideration and debate, and it is
simultaneously a clear and cogent analysis of why and how
such a society cannot come about under capitalism.

To illustrate these points, consider the automobile, which
has had a profound effect on the social and economic structure
of the United States, and with which many Americans have
had a long-standing love affair. Are automobiles desirable? If
the desirable and the desired are synonymous, then the answer
is obvious, for the vast majority of us desire automobiles. But
the continued production and use of automobiles exhausts non-
renewable resources; they generate much waste, are expensive,
require great expenditures for infrastructure development and
maintenance, and contribute significantly to the breakdown of
neighborhoods and communities; all of which suggests that

under many conceptions of the good life, automobiles are not desirable, desire them though we may.

Luntley is not, of course, advocating an immediate prohibition of the manufacture and sale of motor cars (neither am I). What he argues with force and originality, however, is that absent concepts of the good life, and mechanisms for their public airing, no substantive dialogue about automobiles — or education, the media, housing, health care, or any other matter of substance — can occur, and that the economic structures and political ideology of capitalism guarantee that they never will occur.

Concomitant with his critique of capitalism, Luntley offers a solid conceptual analysis of the shortcomings of liberal theories of justice, rights, and equality, and perhaps more important, offers as well a philosophical justification for governmental intervention in private lives that has no taint of totalitarianism, and does not require any dogmatic statements about the nature of the good life itself. It is a new meaning that he gives to socialism, and to the idea of citizenship.

Along the way, Luntley also provides insights on a number of other philosophical issues, ranging from relativism, objectivity, and truth to forms of democracy, the distribution of wealth, and the importance of communities. What links these several discussions together is his central vision of the authority of the good, and I believe he is correct to proceed in this way. All of us, I suspect, hold at least a few things dear enough that we would be willing to die on their behalf, and that we would die for them on the basis of deeply-held moral principles. If this is true, it must be the case that we all do, each in our own way, acknowledge the authority of the good, and that we all do believe there is such a thing as the good life for human beings over and above our individual hopes and fears. To be sure, we are troubled by the fact that there seems to be a plethora of conceptions of the good life, and the blind acceptance of some of those conceptions has led too many people to visit unspeakable horrors on their fellows. But conceptions of the good life can be open as well as closed, and perhaps, among the vast majority of people, those conceptions are not really as divergent as we have been led to believe. In any case, Luntley makes clear that our political activities are and must be grounded in values, but that we cannot compare our conceptions of the good life until and unless we have mechanisms for their articulation, mechanisms that cannot come into play so long as the concepts of individualism and the profit motive structure govern our political interactions.

I have written this Foreword as an American, to fellow Americans. I have done so because the examples given in *The Meaning of Socialism* are drawn from the United Kingdom in which Michael Luntley lives, and for this U. S. edition of his book it seemed important to note at the outset that it is not merely, or even mainly, a critique of the Conservative government of Margaret Thatcher. But by the same token, it is not merely, or mainly, a critique of the Reagan and Bush administrations either. It is a philosophical book, one that should be of equal interest and importance to the Americans — whose name I have appropriated — living north and south of U. S. borders, to Africans, and to Asians as well; in short, to everyone who has a conception of the good life they believe to be valid and true independently of their having it, and who are willing to attend sympathetically to the conceptions of others in order that convergence of all of those conceptions might some day be achieved. Just possibly, the American Dream might be replaced by one that can be shared by all peoples, holding their humanity in common.

April 1990   H. R.
Spring Ridge, Maryland

Preface

This book is about the theory of socialism. It is not a set of prescriptions of how we should go about constructing a socialist society. It is not a policy document outlining a socialist manifesto. It is about something more urgent. Ultimately it is concerned with one central question: Is it ever legitimate to interfere and regulate the market mechanisms of capitalism for some favoured end? Socialists the world over of many different persuasions engage in such interference and regulation and the fundamental problem facing socialists is the lack of confidence that this is legitimate. Such has been the core challenge to socialism across the developed industrial world. Until the challenge is answered no amount of detailed policy prescription will have a lasting effect on the condition of social life in the modern world. In this book I outline the only viable answer to this challenge. I outline the meaning of socialism.

I conceived of the idea for this book after the the 1983 UK election when the Thatcher administration achieved its second term of office. I was impelled to realise the conception after her third electoral success in 1987. I have tried throughout the argument to employ lessons and examples from recent political experience. Political theory is not an intellectual game. It matters terribly and I have tried to engage where it matters and bites in ordinary life as often as possible. But at heart, my concerns here are theoretical, for without a clear theoretical base, our daily concerns rarely ever get properly focussed.

I have been helped in formulating the arguments of this work by many people. The beginning of Mrs Thatcher's third term of office coincided with my introduction to the socialist philosophy group. While not agreeing with many of the group's individual and collective initiatives, I have learnt much from its discussions and have gained from presenting parts of this work to the group on two occassions. For comments, criticisms and suggestions that I can recollect, I thank Richard Bellamy, Ross Brennan, Howard Caygill, Gerry Cohen, Mark Hope, Fred Inglis, Nigel Kemp, Liam O'Sullivan, Phil Wheatley and John Willman. For the past two years I have been fortunate to have David Wiggins as a colleague. The measured calm of his approach to matters of moral and political philosophy has done much to temper my own more headstrong approach even if it is not apparent in these pages. But I have learned much from him and I am grateful for it.

With our universities in disrepair and scholars of every persuasion fleeing the land in such of fresher pastures where the intellectual life is valued for its own sake, I am acutely aware of the debt I owe the British Academy for providing the support, in the form of a post-doctoral research fellowship, that enabled me to write this book. It is a salutary thought that, under the proposed reforms of the universities under market criteria of success, relevance and efficiency, there may soon be a time when the sorts of theoretical pursuits recorded in this book will be erased from our campuses. These are hard times for anyone working outside those fields that satisfy the narrowly philistine preoccupations of our present masters. I wrote this book so that we might have a better notion of how to bring to an end the current barrenness in our society and make plain that the option of doing so is within our grasp.

This book is dedicated to the memory of my father. I was too young to know of his politics, let alone understand them, when he was alive. I now know that he would have approved of this project and hope others may join in our common purpose.

December 1988   M.L.
University College, Oxford

Introduction

Socialism is in crisis. That much at least is clear. And beyond
that is all manner of confusion. This brief book is an attempt to
put together a vision of what socialism might be and become
and of how we might overcome the confusion and the faltering
struggle to keep an alternative agenda going through the
ravages of the renewal of Right-wing politics and theory. My
aim is simply this: to provide a clear but rigorous statement of
the theoretical base and aims of socialism and to do this in a
manner that provides a politics fit to survive and flourish into
the next century. Much is at stake, for if my arguments are
right, if the project fails we will see not just the demise of a
cluster of political parties and the thwarted aspirations of a
sizeable chunk of our polity, we will see the demise of the very
possibility that our society will find a way to live according to
the dictates of our moral senses and reason. A central thesis
advanced in these pages is the identification of socialism with
the possibility of our achieving a society shaped by moral
forces, not by the caprice of Capital. I shall elaborate and
defend this identification shortly. I believe it is right, but I
acknowledge that its correctness vastly raises the stakes in the
attempt to trace the meaning of socialism.

   The task is a philosophical one. What is currently lacking on
the Left is a clear and compelling account of the *ideas* that
underpin socialist policy. The signal achievement of the new
Right and, in the UK, of Mrs Thatcher's government in
particular, has been the way that policy initiatives have all
flowed from a simple consistent vision of the nature of society
and the role of individuals within it. The Right has, for the
moment, achieved a lucid if naïve clarity about the social world
and has derived its policy accordingly to fit the vision. It is this
which has been so conspicuously absent on the Left. In
practical terms, much whining and whingeing has taken the
place of a thoughtful alternative vision. Bereft of ideas, the

1

Left has too often taken to the hackneyed catcalls of class struggle and retreated to the comfort and security of familiar institutions presumed untainted by the advances of the Right. In the UK this has meant a Labour party whose sense of the moral high ground enjoined clinging to the apron strings of the nurses and a National Health Service erroneously presumed inviolable even from the present government.

This will not do. 'Socialism' has come to stand for so many things to so many people that the radical cause against capitalism has been thoroughly blunted. The time is ripe for some hard thinking and blunt speaking. The Left can no longer acquiesce in familiar slogans and wearied thoughts. It must examine its own navel with a rigour and detachment long since lost.

A number of efforts have been made in recent years along this path, but I make no apologies for the definite article in my title. Like any theoretician in this domain, I can offer the following only as an account of *the* right answer. The present disarray on the Left can only be resolved by securely fixing in place the conceptual structure of socialism. What follows is my account of how that structure should be fixed. In this introduction I shall propose some of the key ideas and distinctions that are central to the development of my argument.

1. Initial clarifications

It would be tempting to begin with a well-framed definition of socialism and then proceed to justify the components of the position. We might then conclude with an oration to the glory of the position so outlined. But I am not so tempted. It is no exaggeration to say that socialism is in a mess, and it requires more than a slick definition and supporting argument to put things right. I shall offer a working definition in §5, but first we must review our situation and mark some important distinctions.

One thing that marks socialist thought in the UK is the way people instinctively associate socialism with distinctive *methods* rather than distinctive *goals*. So people associate socialism with centralised state planning, or the nationalisation of key industries and increased direct taxation, rather than with a notion of the sort of society socialists wish to bring about. The reasons for this are, no doubt, largely historical and as much connected with the piecemeal struggle of the British labour movement to gain concessions from Capital as with the intellectual vacuum that too often passes for thought. But whatever the reasons, this concentration on methods not goals is a perversity.

The perversion is twofold. First, the methods that spring so readily to mind are largely discredited and too much linked in the public imagination with the monolithic dullness of a grey paternalistic state apparatus. As Tocqueville noted a long time ago, 'Centralised administration ... perpetuates in the social body a type of administrative drowsiness which the heads of the administration are inclined to call good order and public tranquillity'.[1] Much more serious is the second perversity of the concentration on methods. It is this: It ignores the moral outrage that typically fires socialists.

The ideal socialist, to say nothing of a good many real ones, has a fire in her belly and a moral hymn in her heart. Perhaps not so many can now remember the tune, and the words are long since forgotten, but the centrality of the normative cutting edge to socialism's critique of the status quo cannot be too heavily emphasised. Whatever else is distinctive of socialism it must have, centrally, a morally informed vision of a better life. It must have that cutting edge to its attacks on Capital that comes from commanding the moral high ground. And whether or not we think of this point in terms of the chariots-of-fire or Jerusalem Construction Company version of socialism (from whose work we shall not cease till England's green and pleasant land has been turned over to grand public works for the benefit of all) we must not lose sight of the importance of the moral fire, for there is a very important point here. It is this.

Central to any credible version of socialism must be the idea that there is such a thing as *the good life*. That is to say, there must be a conception of social life, a conception built upon ideas about what things are good and bad irrespective of whether or not many people currently view these things as good or bad. Such a conception tells us something about how we think society *ought* to be, regardless of the way it actually is. And it is

[1] *De la democratie en Amerique*, vol. 1, 158.

this conception of the good life that informs the moral outrage with which socialists criticise the status quo. For if there is one thing that typifies socialists and terrifies their opponents it is that socialists love to interfere. In contrast to the liberal who tries hard to leave well alone and let people decide for themselves on what makes for a good life, the socialist, on seeing the way market mechanisms distribute goods and favours, cannot resist tinkering with the mechanisms to produce some favoured result. Socialists are drawn increasingly from the professional meddling classes, and this is no accident. I shall argue that it is central to socialist activity and theory that there should be more to the good life than the unrestrained pluralism and individualism of liberal theory. It is because of this that socialists interfere with the way the market works. It is because of the idea of there being something called 'the good life' that socialists have a licence for interference.

Let us not be mistaken about the importance of this point: acceptance of it amounts to a radical departure from much accepted political theory. And although this means that we risk making many enemies and losing a good few friends along the way, I am convinced of the profound importance of this point. Of course, if we are bold enough to admit our role as interfering promoters of the good, we must acknowledge that we are desperately in need of a *model of interference*. The models that spring readily to mind – the busy-bodying do-gooder and the totalitarian despot – are clearly unpalatable. We need to know what model of interference can be legitimised by our notion of the good life. I shall introduce the model shortly and expand it in Chapter 1. But to show that this business about the good life and a model of interference is in deadly earnest, here are two ways of pressing the idea of the importance of the notion of the good for the development of socialism: first by its role in defending a concept of social justice, and second by its role in contrasting socialism with liberalism.

2. The good and social justice

With what right do we say that someone has been wronged when they suffer unemployment and its consequences even though their fate was not the conscious choice of any one agent? This is a common enough scenario in our society.

Decisions are made with no intentional bearing upon the lives of others and yet, through the hidden-hand mechanisms of the market, someone or other eventually suffers as a consequence. Equally pertinent is the way that the complexities of society bring about unintended benefits for individuals. The individual followers of pop music have no intention of making their idol fabulously rich, but the cumulative effect of ticket and record purchases does just that. The entrepreneur has no intention of making this or that worker unemployed with all the consequent financial and emotional hardship that that brings; nevertheless the outcome of her actions may well spell disaster in numerous households. In both cases there is a strong impulse to modify such cumulative outcomes by appeal to a notion of social justice: fabulous riches should be redistributed through the taxation system, a safety net of welfare and restraints should be established to assist the unintended casualties of complex market decisions. But this impulse needs justification. Why are we right to interfere?

Our attitudes to such impulses divide into two fundamentally different approaches to questions about justice, which we might call the *historical* and *end-state* accounts of justice. On the historical approach, justice is a purely deontological concept; that is to say, it is a concept, like that of a *right*, which works solely as a constraint upon the way people act. On this approach, a distribution of goods in society is just if it has been arrived at by processes that conform to the appropriate structural constraints. So, for example, in the case of the pop star's wealth, if all the fans genuinely owned the money with which they bought their concert tickets in the first place, and assuming that they are entitled to do with their possessions as they see fit, then the fact that in purchasing tickets they unwittingly brought about fabulous wealth for one individual is neither here nor there with regard to the justice of the consequent distribution of wealth. Similarly with the case of the worker made unemployed. Providing no agent has acted intentionally to harm the worker, the worker cannot complain that she has been wronged, only that she is the unfortunate recipient of a bad hand dealt by market forces.[1]

[1] A well-known recent version of an historical account of justice is Robert Nozick's entitlement theory of justice in *Anarchy, State and Utopia* (Oxford 1975), which in turn picks up features from a tradition going back to Locke.

These accounts of the examples contrast with those that depend upon an end-state conception of justice. In such a case, justice is not simply a matter of how a particular distribution came about, it is also concerned with the end-state pattern of the distribution. There may well be constraints on how distributions of goods come about, but there is also an element to the concept of justice which is concerned with the resulting pattern of distribution. Any theory which embodies an egalitarian or a redistributive element to its account of justice will be an end-state account of justice.[1] When socialists employ a notion of social justice in criticising the suffering brought about by unemployment or the inequity of massive wealth, they are appealing to an end-state notion of justice. And it is the notion of the good of this end-state that alone can license the socialist interference.

But socialists are faced with a problem here, for we live in a political culture which is predominantly disposed towards historical notions of justice and opposed to there being scope for substantive debate about a concept of the good that might inform a richer, end-state, concept of justice. The contrast here is this: Do we think that the determination of goods should be left wholly to the choice of individuals fixing goods for themselves, or do we think that there is what we might call a *social dimension to the good*? If we think the former, society is no more than the flux of individuals chasing their own ideas of the good and, providing no one deliberately acts to harm another, if someone suffers harm that is no more than an unfortunate side-effect of the complex matrix of individual goods-seekers. And, on this option, the resulting unemployment and massive unevenness of wealth distribution is not an injustice.

In contrast there is the option of saying that there is a social dimension to the good. The good is something over and above what the various individuals in society happen to seek after at any one time, it is something that takes within its compass the way things are for society as a whole and not just for individuals. This is a radical idea. A central problem for

---

[1] John Rawls' *A Theory of Justice* (Harvard 1972) is the most celebrated recent attempt at such an account.

socialists lies in coming to terms with just how radical this idea is.

The left has for too long been impressed by the agenda of liberalism in terms of which we think of ourselves as isolated moral consciousnesses. On this agenda there is no space for the idea of the good as a collective notion, something about which we need to argue together and construct between us. The agenda allows only for the private individual fancies and goods that flourish within the minimal constraints of theories of rights which, in turn, lay down the ground rules by which seekers after goods avoid collisions in the frantic market place of social life. The demise of the notion of the good as something which transcends individual choice is well measured by the advance in our history of the importance of theories of rights.

Where we have a substantive notion of the good we have less need for a theory of rights to carve out our moral space. In a society in which there exists a substantive notion of the good life it is not necessary to protect individuals with the abstract barriers of rights, for their place in society is marked by their shared grasp of the good. Take a homely, but sharp, example. The notion of family life is often thought to embody certain ideas of the good. The family is, often enough, the seat of our moral life. Being a parent automatically carries certain obligations and ideas of the good – what a good parent is like. But the disruption and fragmentation of our ideas, indeed our very language of the good, has now reached the point where this is no longer so common.

The extent of the collapse of shared ideas of the good can be measured by the increase in the language of rights. As the moral sphere shaped by the good collapses so talk of rights steps in to protect individuals from the ensuing moral vacuum. And at this point in the closing years of the twentieth century, the collapse of the moral life is nearly complete. We now find that it is necessary to invoke the concept of *children's rights*. Being a child no longer guarantees a shared role and conception of the good with one's parent. The moral space in which a young life may find comfort and recognition is no longer automatically provided by a shared good life, it must be protected by the abstract claims of rights against those who now, rather than being cast as partners in a common moral life, are cast as potential adversaries: these people are your parents. The sphere of the moral life, a common good, has now collapsed to the point forecast in liberal political theory: the good extends no further than the limits of the self-interested individual.

It is amazing how often this strikes people as the natural starting point for moral and political theory. Our problem is always that of justifying a concern that reaches *out* from the individual to encompass others: the problem is one of justifying altruism. But this gets things dangerously the wrong way around. The problem is much more fundamental. How are we to revive a political culture, an idea of a civil society, in which we find our moral place given within a tradition rather than grasping a place within a moral free-for-all? I shall argue that the fundamental question for socialists is not how to justify an altruistic concern for others, how to work out from the isolated moral agent to encompass others; the problem is how to rethink, how to learn a language and political culture that immediately and unproblematically makes the lives of others already part of a shared concern and notion of the good life. Until we can do that, no amount of altruism will do any good. And, of course, when once we have done that, our actions are no longer interferences, but a collaboration in the attempt to write the story of the good life together.

This is so often misunderstood. If you think that all would be well if only we could tap people's natural altruism, you have already lost the argument. That remark can seem unduly pessimistic, but it is not; for what it stresses is the fundamental problem of legitimation that faces socialism. Consider the following. Suppose a socialist party finds enough altruists in society to get itself elected and then sets about redistributing wealth. With what legitimacy does it take higher taxes from those of the wealthy who do not succumb to the altruistic drive? This is a serious and fundamental question. It is not enough to suppose that an electoral majority legitimates a 'screw the rich' policy unless you are happy to forfeit any legitimate complaints when, if the tables are turned, a succeeding government finds the electoral resources to screw the poor. There is more to politics than such crude power play. If we think that screwing the poor is actually wrong, that it affronts some notion of social justice – the social dimension to the good – then taxing the rich must have some good to it. It is not just an advantageous ploy. Legitimacy cuts both ways. If we have legitimate complaints against the Thatcher government which has, at least, won three elections in a row, we must have legitimacy for plans for the redistribution of wealth.

Such legitimacy will not come from a programme that starts inwards with the individual looking out to others and trying to bring them within the compass of altruism. We must first refashion the traditions of community and the good life that alone can bring us and others within a common moral sphere. The importance of the notion of the good life is further revealed when we pursue the difference between socialism and liberalism.

3. Socialism vs. liberalism

Acceptance of the centrality of the notion of the good life for socialism can be contrasted with the typical liberal position. Suppose we are deliberating on whether or not to implement some policy – say, to start a hospital building programme. We want to know, in part, whether it is a good thing that the building programme be undertaken. One way of answering the question is to discover the preferences of all the individuals in society with regard to the issue and treat the answer to our question as a function of individual desires and preferences. Let me call such an approach a method that endorses an *economism about values*. It treats questions of value, questions about what is good, as a function of what individuals happen to desire. Just as the economist computes the demand for, say, soap powder X from a matrix of individual preferences for X, so this approach computes the good society from a matrix of individual conceptions of good.

Two things are worth noting about this economism with values. First, acceptance of such economism entails a potent form of individualism in social theory. It commits us to the claim that the only source of value lies with the individual: if we want to know whether or not something is valuable we must look to the desires of individuals. But secondly, this individualism means that acceptance of economism about values entails that there is no such thing as the good life. There is only the plurality of different conceptions of good found

among different individuals. These two points are constitutive
of classical liberal theory.

If there is no such thing as the good life, the most that
political theory can hope to do is to articulate a structure of
constraints within which individuals can be left to determine
their own conceptions of the good life. Political theory then
becomes synonymous with a theory of rights which carves out
the space in which, and the rules by which, individuals are left
free to shape their own notions of the good. This is
characteristic, if not definitive, of liberal political theory – the
Right takes precedence over the Good. (In philosophical jargon,
this is known as the precedence of deontology – the theory of
rights and duties – over teleology – the theory of good.) And
upon this precedence of theory about rights over theory of good
is built the whole rhetorical façade about the dignity and
freedom of the individual who, afloat in a moral vacuum, sets
about creating values and goods unaided and unimpeded by
the will of others.

Socialism must reject all this. For suppose a socialist
accepted economism about values. Suppose, that is, that she
accepted that the good life amounted to no more than the
condition of individuals having their preferences satisfied. This
then amounts to acceptance of a free market in values. That
being so, the most that the state or any political party can offer
to do within our polity is to guard the structural deontological
framework which protects this free market. What such
agencies cannot do is to protest if, at any particular point in
time, a majority are content with the operation of the free
market in values. A socialist party could then have no
legitimacy for protest at a society with an electoral majority of
contented capitalists who did not want to distribute their
wealth to the disadvantaged. In such a case there would be no
foundation for the thought that, despite the contentment of its
members, such a society would be wrong.

It is important that the problem posed here is a problem of
legitimation, it is not a practical problem of how to go about
securing the means for some redistribution of wealth. The
fundamental problem with which the argument of this book is
concerned is a problem about the legitimacy of interference for
the good of society. As such it is not an argument about the
viability of, say, a progressive taxation policy should a socialist

government be elected. Too often people are deflected by considering the question of *how* we should interfere without giving an answer to the question of whether, if we *do* interfere, we have legitimate licence to interfere. That is the central philosophical question that socialism must answer before any of its particular prescriptions can be put into effect. It is this legitimation issue with which I shall be centrally concerned. And note that it is not simply a philosophical matter with no impact on political practice, for it is the directness of Mrs Thatcher's attack on the legitimacy of socialist interference rather than on particular practices of interference that has left her opposition so ineffectual. It has been her central challenge to deny the legitimacy of socialist interference and her championing of the lone moral agent that has given the grounding for her claim that socialism is dead. If socialism is to live into the next century the legitimation issue must be settled. It is central. I shall pursue the arguments in support of the centrality of the concept of the good in settling the legitimation issue in Chapter 1, but I think there is sufficient *prima facie* plausibility for the point now.

So let us accept this claim that socialism must have a central concern with the concept of the good life, for this alone looks to provide an answer to the legitimation problem. Let us view socialism as the antithesis of the liberal idea that there is no such thing as the good life, merely the flux of individuals in a moral vacuum freely putting together a plurality of conceptions of the good. We can sum this up with the following principle, acceptance of which I shall take as constitutive of socialism:

> *The Good Principle*: There is more to the achievement of the good life than the satisfaction of individuals' actual preferences.

At the moment I have given no argument for this other than to note that its endorsement seems to be a prerequisite for using the concept of the good to solve the legitimation problem. Endorsement of the Good Principle provides socialism with the normative cutting edge to its critiques of contemporary society. It is what makes it a philosophy of interference. It provides socialism with a foundational moral concern to bring about something that I am calling the good life. Socialists can then criticise society not only because people are not getting what they want, but because they are not getting what it is good to get, regardless of whether or not they actually have a present desire for it. Acceptance of the Good Principle commits us to a rejection of liberalism and its economism about values. It commits us to an anti-individualism about moral values that I think is central to any worthwhile socialism. But it also looks to commit us to a distasteful paternalism. This is not so.

Supposing that the brief sketch so far is right, there appear to be two glaring faults. First, acceptance of the Good Principle seems to smack too much of paternalism, and secondly, amidst this highly abstract discussion just what are the elements of a socialist conception of the good life? The second point I shall answer in §5, but first let me deflect the charge of paternalism.

4. Socialism: a model of interference

The individualism of the liberal position leaves the determination of the good to the choice of each and every agent unencumbered by the decisions of others. In the liberal model the ultimate authority for the good lies with each individual. Acceptance of the Good Principle seems to take away the authority residing in the individual and give it to another agent. This is a mistake, but the charge of paternalism and totalitarianism will come so easily that it is worth unpacking carefully.

Liberals will do all in their power to avoid telling another person what is for their good. They believe that each should be free to determine her own good. Liberals are tolerant to a fault. However, endorsing the Good Principle does *not* entail that one should adopt the posture of one who claims to *know* what is good for another. Endorsing the Good Principle does commit us to acknowledging that we do not have ultimate authority over what is good, but it does not mean that that authority is given to another individual or, for that matter, to a collective agent like a party. What it does commit us to is this: It commits us to acknowledging the *Authority of the Good*. The point of the Good Principle is a metaphysical point, it is the claim that there is such a thing as the good over and above what individuals might happen to think is the good. But that is all. As yet nothing is presupposed about who, if anyone, knows what the good is. All that is presupposed is that there is such a thing. The authority of the good is not the authority of another agent, it is the authority of the truth, the objective account of the good life – that is what we must defer to, not other individuals.

Consider an analogy here. In our scientific enquiries we believe that there is such a thing as the truth about the way the world works. Now, acceptance of this belief could be expressed in terms of a truth principle, namely:

There is more to the achievement of scientific truth than the satisfaction of present scientists' actual puzzlements.

It would be ludicrous to think that acceptance of this metaphysical point, that there is such a thing as the truth over and above what individuals might happen to think is the truth, commits us to a view about who has access to the truth and how. Indeed the authority of truth to which scientists must defer commits us to the idea that if one scientist or set of scientists sets itself up as a vanguard of privileged enquirers after the truth, we would contest its claim to be engaged in enquiry after objective truth. Objective truth does not admit of privileged access like that.

The scientific deference to the authority of truth does not amount to obsequiousness to some petrified set of eternal verities, nor to the command of a set of high priests of science. That would be the very antithesis of deference to the authority of truth. Deferring to the authority of truth requires a certain attitude, a certain methodology comprising a commitment to experimentation, repeatability of tests and objective measurement of results before the benchmark of our common experience. These may be tall ideals to live up to, but it is such methodological requirements that are implicated in bowing to the authority of truth. The same applies in bowing to the authority of the good.

The notion of the good life is the notion of the truth about what constitute goods and evils for human beings. And, just as in the scientific analogy, so deference to the authority of the good, far from being a start on the slippery slope to totalitarianism, is the best guard we have against such terrors. Totalitarianism comes about when some individual or group seizes the power to force its conception of the good upon others and to stifle the free argument and experimentation necessary for true deference to the authority of the good. We know, broadly speaking, how to go about satisfying the methodological requirements that make for truth-seeking in science. The traditions of community and the good life which I have suggested are required for us to engage in a substantive dialogue about the good have been largely forgotten. We know how to argue about the truth in science, but we have lost the will and skill to debate about substantive goods in politics. Instead we have become enamoured of the clamour of rights and the jostling of position of self-interested individuals pressing for ever more room to pursue their individual goods.

The model of interference we require, then, must appeal to a notion of the possibility of *argument about the good*. The predominant trend in moral and political philosophy, and in our culture at large, is to deny that substantive argument about ends is possible. Relativism rules and liberalism has made tolerance of others and their creeds, however perverse, a leading principle. We seldom now dare to criticise another's moral choice, or actively to promote our own. Instead we are encouraged to shrink within our moral shells and pursue a moral masturbation of private goods and delights. We no longer *talk* about the things that matter, but mumble in inaudible whispers. Our model of interference must unlock this inhibited whittering and release a raucous moral chatter. We interfere then, not by imposition, not by reaching out across the liberal moral void and imposing our private goods upon the will of another, but legitimately when we engage with another in substantive argument about ends and goals. We interfere when we find the scope for a debate about ultimate ends, when we shake off the pussy-footed timidity of liberal relativism and engage in a discourse that sets itself to seek out the truth, a discourse that is undertaken in deference to the authority of the good. And although to the liberal that looks like interference, it is, of course, nothing like it. It is life led according to the force of moral values, life shaped by the good. A necessary precondition for such a life is that we should come to the argument *already members of a moral community, or tradition*. Much of the argument of this book will be concerned with defending the concept of a tradition as the repository of the good life, the thing which allows substantive moral argument to flourish.

5. Defining socialism

If socialism is to be built upon a concern for the good life, an objective account of goods for humans, we are immediately faced with an embarrassing reticence from most socialist writers when it comes to offering an account of the good. The importance of the Good Principle noted above may capture much of what the traditional opposition socialists feel for liberal theory, but until we have some specific account of the goods taken to be part of the good life are we not a thousand miles short of socialism? It is in answer to this question that I introduce the central theoretical claim that I shall develop in the chapters to come.

The claim is this: Socialism is not a moral theory which offers a particular vision of the good life, instead it is a theory about how the good life is possible. It is, in short, a theory about the conditions necessary for creating a society in which our lives are shaped by moral values – we defer to the authority of the good – rather than a society in which our moral traditions have been erased by forces inimical to the moral life. And part of this theory about the conditions necessary for the good life provides the leading critical aspect of socialism. That part is the claim that it is capitalism which has been largely responsible for the destruction of the conditions necessary for the good life.

So we have two complementary theses that are central to the account of socialism I have to offer. First, there is an account of what has to be the case in order that the moral values may flourish and shape our society. Secondly, there is an account of how the emergence and continuation of capitalist modes of production have disrupted and thwarted the moral life. This way of understanding what socialism is about is in contrast to the common unreflective grasp of socialism.

Most people who count themselves socialists do so out of a sense of moral outrage at the way goods and services are distributed in society. They find that society is organised in a way that is anathema to certain values they hold. Theirs is an empirical socialism that arises from the way the world confronts particular values they hold. It is also a first-order socialism. What I mean by this is that such socialism is built upon an antecedent acceptance of first-order moral imperatives. A first-order socialist starts with some such value as equality (however interpreted) and, in the light of this, has a picture of how the world could be a better place if that value were employed in the social and economic management of things. We might, unkindly, call this Travel Brochure socialism, or TB socialism for short.

The TB socialist starts with particular first-order moral imperatives and pieces together a travel guide to the *El Dorado* of the socialist paradise to which she would like to sell us all a one-way ticket. There are many things that are disturbing about TB socialism, not least the fervour with which such socialists, like all good travel agents, describe half-built resorts. But the chief difficulty, which I shall develop in Chapter 1, is this. It can provide no legitimacy to critiques or interventions when others disagree about the location and desirability of the supposed resort. In short, TB socialism is far too economical with values. If we are not to endorse economism with values we must do more than start with values dear to us: we must have a means for showing them preferable to others on display.

The TB socialist pins her banners of liberty, comradeship and equality to the masthead and implores the electorate to join the happy throng of travellers down the route to the socialist good life. They know where they are going before the charabanc leaves. I have not yet outlined the goods which I think make up the socialist good life, for I do not believe we know, or need to know, what they are. And this is because the socialism on offer in this book is a *second-order socialism*.

The first-order, or TB socialist, has a conception of the good life and seeks to enable herself and others to live that life. The second-order socialist has a more fundamental concern, a concern best expressed negatively in a critique of capitalism. It is this: *The fault of capitalism and the free-market economy is not that it fails on this or that particular value that constitutes part of the socialist good life; rather it fails because it systematically obstructs the possibility for living the good life. Capitalism fails because it stands in the way of the construction of the good life whatever final shape it may have.* That is the key to the account of socialism that I shall offer. In summary:

Socialism is the belief that only by dismantling the economisation of human relationships found under capitalism will we be able to construct the good life.

Of course, this is to put the definition of socialism at a very abstract level, although I believe it captures an idea central to many socialist thinkers. But the abstraction does not matter. What matters is the idea that instead of thinking of socialism defined in terms of some static conception of a desirable endstate, we are to think of it as a dynamic philosophy concerned with the process of bringing about the construction of the good life.

To revert to the earlier analogy with science, socialism is not defined in terms of the goal, the truth about human goods which we seek: it is defined in terms of the activity and attitude required in order to make such truth accessible. Socialism starts from an account of the kind of argument required to deliver substantive results about the good.

So the central concern for socialism is not the pursuit of this or that particular value or good, but the pursuit of the good life in general untrammelled by the distortions of capitalistic economic structures. The central concern is not then a theory of particular goods, but a concern that the good life be attainable.

Of course, it is such an abstract starting point that one might wonder why any of this should be called 'socialism'. That is a fair question, to which there are two answers. First, the sort of critique of capitalism that I shall offer and the sorts of results favoured by the critique will turn out to have much in common with familiar socialist ideals. I cannot guarantee in advance that I shall be able to deliver all the values socialists have cherished, but then I am not a utopian. The second answer is more important. It is this.

What is *social* about the socialism on offer in this book is the foundation of our moral values. In contrast to the rampant individualism of liberalism, which grants unfettered freedom to individuals to construct whatever value systems they please, I shall argue that the only real grounding for values and the good life must reside in our communities and the traditions with which they supply us. We have been gripped too long by the moral vacuum of the Hayekian rhetoric that says that no one can ever legitimately instruct us as to our own good and that we are sovereign over our own moral lives, that we have authority over the good, not *vice versa*. But this is nonsense, and we must say so loudly and often.

It is nonsense because anyone concerned for the sense of moral value that can inform and shape our lives must realise that for such values to count they cannot be grounded in isolated moral consciousnesses. Too often we assume that our moral bonds to others can come only from within, from some contract or bargain struck in a moral vacuum. But it is not like that. When we find ourselves impelled to act because how things are for another impinges directly upon how things are for us, this comes from our first having a sense of shared traditions. It comes, as it can only come, from without, from the sense of community and tradition in which we confront our neighbours. The only genuine ground for moral values, the only genuine hope for a truly civil society, must come from our shared traditions of thought and feeling that are carried by the communities in which we live. Such things cannot be created *ab initio* from the vacuum of classical liberal theory. We do not, in the first instance, stand alone.

And this matters. It matters because until we can protect our communities from the onslaught of Capital chasing its profit motive, we can kiss goodbye to any credible notion of the good life and a civil polity. It is the unfettered pursuit of the logic of capital that has so dislocated our communities and, with them, our sense of moral, political and, often, familial purpose. And now, if despite this radical challenge to the orthodoxy of liberal political theory you still wonder why I call this 'socialism', I can only reply, 'Just wait and see.'

Of course there will be much of the traditional socialist panoply of favourite concerns that *is* missing. For example, I shall give little room to the concept of class, but in the late twentieth-century climate of post-industrial capitalism I can hardly fear that this is a failing. Certainly in the UK the concept of class has been too much a cultural notion, rather than a specifically political concept. It has been too much bound up with the 'Ee, lad, tha doesn't know what poverty's abowt' syndrome to offer much instructive analysis of what socialists should be thinking about in the closing years of this century. I feel no guilt in trying to shake off the corporatist cloth-capped unionised concept of class-warfare in my attempt to describe a socialism that can build futures for our children, not rosy nostalgia for our grandparents.

6. Overview of the argument

I have now introduced some of the ideas and distinctions that will be crucial in the argument to come. The plan of the argument is this. In Chapter 1 I expound and defend the identification of socialism with an account of what is required in order that the good life be possible. I give some account of what it is that is required for this: namely, the social base of the good life in the traditions handed down by our communities. Chapter 2 picks up the critique of capitalism first offered in Chapter 1, that capitalism is responsible for the fragmentation of our traditions. This is developed in contrast to the claim that it is the ownership relations found in capitalism that are its fault. The central line of the argument is that being a moral agent, as opposed to being an economic agent, requires deference to the authority of the good. For only then are we able to uncover the criteria for moral agency. Under capitalism, the criteria of moral agency are supplanted by the criteria of economic agency. In order to re-establish the scope for moral agency in our polity, in order to empower people into moral agency, the profit motive that fuels a capitalist economy must be regulated and controlled in order to enable the criteria for moral agency to be articulated. The argument generalises to other kinds of agency. For all sorts of agencies in our society, including institutional agencies like the media, there are criteria of successful agency which need to be established and protected against the criteria that come into play when such agencies are required to bow to criteria of economic success. In total, these various criteria of agency for people and institutions define our civil society. Civil society can only come into being when the criteria of economic agency which capitalism emphasises are made subservient to those non-profit-oriented criteria of agency which define our civil society. In short, the argument is an argument about the conditions of moral agency and of how these conditions require the dethronement of the conditions of economic agency contrary to the spirit of capitalism. The argument applies to non-economic notions of agency other than moral agency.

An obvious response to the general line of argument I develop is that, with its emphasis on the notion of traditions and the reference groups as the foundation of the moral life, why is this not merely a statement of conservatism, not socialism? This is a good question, and I answer it in Chapter 3. There I first show why the idea of an objective notion of the good is not a silly idea, and then I develop a concept of ideology with which we can criticise and emend our traditions. *That* is what differentiates the position here from conservatism, for I offer a dynamic account of the process of critique of our traditions as we strive to develop a non-ideological account of the good life, an account unclouded by the distorting effects of capitalism.

Chapters 1 to 3 develop the main positive elements of the position. Chapter 4 rebuts the charge that I have dangerously ignored the concept of freedom. I there show that the concepts of freedom and choice, as they surface in libertarian arguments, are worthless. Chapter 5 considers whether another familiar concept from the liberal tradition, that of justice, has been unduly neglected in the development of the position, and I conclude that it has not. Chapter 6 tackles, all too briefly, the concept of democracy and the rule of law and the question how they should be handled by a socialist. Genuinely difficult problems arise for a socialist committed to the idea of an objective account of the good life. For example, should we break the law if the law does not enshrine the good? I conclude that we should. Finally, Chapter 7 considers some of the peculiarities of socialism in the UK. My aim is not policy pronouncement: it is to articulate the theoretical space that accommodates some fresh agenda in which others may develop policy. But ultimately some of the measure of the position I develop must depend on the quality and quantity of policy proposals thereby created.

1

Markets, Values and Traditions

I have suggested that socialism is typified by a central concern for what I have called the good life. In this respect, socialism stands in stark contrast to the predominant liberal traditions in political theory and practice. Liberalism has taught us an ethics of politeness in which we refrain from proposing or commenting on substantive ends. Our need now is to refashion the practices of moral discourse. We need to uncover the ground rules and preconditions of moral agency. Once this is done we can set about replacing the economic agency of capitalism with the moral agency of socialism. In this chapter I shall provide the arguments to support these points and show what is required in order to make the concept of the good life viable. I start with the arguments to support the centrality of the good. There are two main arguments for this, a negative and a positive. I start with the negative argument.

1. Two kinds of market socialism

A new breed of socialism has been fashionable of late. It is called market socialism.[1] Market socialists have argued that, providing market mechanisms deliver beneficial outcomes, socialists should embrace the workings of the market. As an economic argument there is much plausibility to this. In their opposition to an old-style bigoted championship of state ownership and planning market socialists have caught the mood of the moment. Their critical point, that markets are, often enough, as likely to be conducive to socialist ends as traditional state ownership and planning, is correct. However,

[1] For a good discussion of this trend see *Market Socialism: whose choice?*, Fabian Society pamphlet no. 516 (London 1986), ed. Ian Forbes.

21

this observation is a thin foundation on which to embrace an extended use of market mechanisms.

In the first place, it is obvious that the viability of market socialism depends crucially on what is meant by 'beneficial outcomes'. This is an obvious point, but for all that it needs making. One person's beneficial outcome is, often enough, another person's economic catastrophe. It seems plausible then to suppose that the viability of market socialism depends on the prior acceptance of what constitutes a beneficial outcome. And that can only emerge from some account of what outcomes of distribution are good, and what are bad. An account of the good is presupposed for the smooth operation of market socialism.

It would be helpful here if we distinguished between two sorts of market socialists, which I shall call the naïve and the sophisticated versions of the position. By the naïve market socialists I mean those who do no more than advocate mixed strategies in handling the economy. This variant amounts only to a plea for the viability of market mechanisms as a means for realising particular goals. It goes no further than the observation that, in many spheres of social and economic life, market mechanisms are more efficient than centrally planned mechanisms in achieving some desired goal. Naïve market socialism is hardly a major theoretical advance on the left. It might have taken untold courage to shake off the dogma of the infallibility of central state planning, but as a theoretical statement it is wholly dependent on a prior account of what distributional results are desirable. It depends on a prior account of the good.

This is in contrast to a sophisticated market socialism. Here I mean a position which attempts to build a theoretical advance for socialism upon market mechanisms. This is a position that sees market mechanisms as themselves sufficient, without an antecedent account of the good, to define a viable socialism. Indeed the sophisticated market socialist believes that neutrality on the subject of what the good life is like is a bonus for socialism. This is a mistake, and a major one at that.

While the broad movement that goes under the label of market socialism received most of its impetus from the economic observation that, with sufficient constraints on, for example, ownership, the market could be left to deliver socialist results, there have been attempts to embrace the more sophisticated version. Two of these are instructive.

First, Brian Barry has attempted to define socialism in a way that, while not specifically addressed as a version of market socialism, embodies the neutrality about the good life that I am taking as characteristic of sophisticated market socialism.[1] In the terms of my Introduction, he espouses an economism about values. He defines socialism as the *collective* attempt to overcome undesirable consequences of individual action. That is, whatever your account of which consequences of market mechanisms are desirable and which undesirable, as long as a society acts collectively to mitigate the latter, it is socialist. Such a position endorses market mechanisms and is deliberately neutral on what count as desirable or undesirable consequences of the market so long as it is collective action which is employed to counter the undesirable. Indeed the neutrality on the account of the good amounts to endorsing a free market in conceptions of the good – what I have called 'economism about values'.

The failure of Barry's definition of socialism is obvious. Without giving up the neutrality on the good, by Barry's definition Mrs Thatcher would be a socialist if she pursued a policy of collective action against undesirable consequences of the market. And, as all major industrial societies, by their very complexity, have to pursue *some* collective strategies, Mrs Thatcher is then a socialist! This is nonsense, and rather dangerous nonsense. Such economism about values lacks critical bite.[2]

A more promising approach to a sophisticated market socialism seems at first to come from attempts made in recent years to locate the theoretical base of socialism in terms of claims of freedom and claims of rights. Such deontological claims are custom-made for neutrality about the good life. But when the approach is inspected, it turns out to presuppose the very concern with the notion of the good that it tries to avoid.

[1] Brian Barry, 'Socialism today', Inaugural Lecture delivered at the London School of Economics, 3 December 1987.
[2] Barry accepts that what flows from his definition depends on what we take the undesirable consequences to be, but has said (in conversation) that the desirable is, as with Mill, to be identified with the desired. This is why it is correct to call his position one of an economism about values.

2. A misplaced faith in freedom

Many people have been concerned at the way the Right has highjacked the concept of freedom in recent debate. The concern is legitimate. The concept of freedom is too often debased to that of economic freedom, the unfettered power to pursue the profit motive free from as many social and political controls as possible. Coupled with this advocacy of freedom is the simple faith that the hidden-hand mechanisms of the market will provide sufficient wealth and means of distribution to bring benefit to all. Now, it is not axiomatic that unrestricted pursuit of the profit motive and faith in hidden-hand mechanisms are bad things, but it would not be incautious to suppose, for the moment, that they are not things socialists typically value or should value. And, of course, when socialists have picked up the banner of freedom, it has not been one with such a Hayekian ancestry.

The account of the theoretical base of socialism presented recently in the *New Statesman* is a good case in point.[1] Drawing on the contributions found there we can piece together the following train of thought:

(1) Freedom is central to any socialist philosophy.

(2) Freedom is important because lack of it inhibits our ability to pursue the good life (with no presumptions about what constitutes the good life).

(3) Lack of freedom can be caused not only by intentional obstructions to agency, but also by the operation of the free market, state organisations, monopolies, etc.

(4) (3) is true because the free market, state organisations, etc., can cause the frustration of basic needs.

Now (1) to (4) express a common line of thought among the British Labour Left.[2] But, if left at that, this line of thought is thoroughly misleading, for it distracts attention from the need

---

[1] See the special edition of the *New Statesman* on the future of socialism for 6 March 1987 and the articles by Hirst, Le Grand and Plant.

[2] As well as the academics in the *New Statesman* pages, such a view is found in the writings of leading Labour politicians; see both Bryan Gould's *Freedom and Socialism* (Basingstoke 1985) and Roy Hattersley's *Freedom and Choice* (London 1987).

to address the question of what constitutes the good life, a matter the successful resolution of which is actually presupposed by the viability of the above line of thought.

The above line of thought is misleading in the following way. (2) reveals that the concept of freedom appealed to is something like the familiar notion of positive freedom. It is certainly not the negative notion of economic freedom championed by Hayek. It is not negative freedom *from* that matters to these socialists, but freedom *to* lead the good life. But that immediately makes the concept of freedom secondary to the account of the good life. Freedom is not an end in itself, but a means – perhaps a necessary means – for achieving the good life. This is only made more evident in claim (3). For if we can suffer unfreedom when no intentional agency interferes with choices, but rather when market forces, state action and monopoly power inhibit choices, it can only be because these things act against some goal of ours that is antecedently acknowledged as a good. *It is the requirements of the good life which ground such claims of unfreedom when our options are restricted in this way.* If it were only restrictions imposed by other subjects that mattered, then, of course, freedom could be counted as an end in itself and we would have, as central, something like the negative concept of economic freedom. That is precisely not the sort of concept such writers appeal to. But a richer notion of freedom which allows that we can be imprisoned by things like market forces must have some account of the good life which can justify this talk of interference with our freedom when no one is interfering.

So, despite the appeal of the idea of recapturing the concept of freedom, if the attack is to work it presupposes that we have some account of the good life. We cannot afford to remain neutral on this or we forfeit our claim to speak of unfreedoms in the sorts of cases that distinguish the socialist use of the notion of freedom from the Right's minimalist notion of economic freedom, the negative freedom to be left to do whatever one likes regardless of the unintended consequences.

Further, if we can, on occasion, be imprisoned by such impersonal things as market forces, then not only do we need an antecedent account of the good life the loss of which justifies talk of imprisonment, we also need the idea that such a good life is *objectively* good. This may not seem so apparent, but the argument for it is this.

It is important to bear in mind that we are considering claims of unfreedom in which no intentional agency brings about the subject's loss of freedom. So we are not concerned with cases where subject K has her freedom impaired by the action of another subject. Rather, the case is one where K has a claim of loss of freedom that arises from impersonal forces: for example, market forces. Call the former kind of case 'intentional unfreedom' and the latter 'impersonal unfreedom'. Now, contrast two situations in both of which some aspect of K's freedom is impaired. In the first case it is intentionally impaired through the actions of another subject, in the second K suffers impersonal unfreedom. Suppose the impairment is to do with K's freedom of expression. The first example might be one where K is deliberately stopped from expressing her views by the actions of politically motivated editors. The second example would be of a situation where K's freedom of expression was impaired by, say, her poverty which effectively took the opportunity to get her opinions broadcast out of her reach.

Now, if we assume that freedom of expression is not objectively good, but only subjectively good, the assessment of the two situations varies. To say that freedom of expression is only subjectively a good is to say that its goodness amounts only to the subject's *thinking* that it is good. Therefore, if a subject has her freedom of expression impaired but does not count that a loss, no harm has been done. In contrast, if freedom of expression is objectively a good, regardless of how a subject counts the loss of this freedom, harm is done when it is impaired.

In the situation of intentional unfreedom, in which K's freedom of expression is deliberately impaired, this can still be criticised whether or not we count the loss as an objective or subjective harm. For even if we count the loss as a subjective harm for K, we can still appeal to more abstract deontological concepts of the inviolability of rights and an individual's moral space, and of the dignity that accrues to an individual unhindered by other individuals. Our basic deontology of rights carves out a framework of moral space the infringement of which is counted immoral without need to appeal to the particular good within an individual's set of goals that is impaired by a violation of moral space. That is why it does not matter, for our assessment of the wrongness of intentional unfreedoms, whether or not we attribute an objective or subjective goodness to the goal that is impaired.

With impersonal unfreedom the case is different. Suppose we take K's restricted freedom of expression as only a subjective harm; that is, it is a harm only because K thinks that it is a harm – it would not be a harm if K were content with the restriction. In this case, because the harm has not been done as a deliberate act by another agent but is rather the consequence of impersonal forces, we have no grounds on which to count the restriction a bad thing, given the assumption of the subjectivity of the harm. For in the impersonal case we cannot appeal to the abstract deontology of rights etc. in order to count the situation as bad. For in the impersonal case there has been no violation by one agent of another's moral space. All that K can say is that her moral space has contracted, but there is no one to whom she can complain. Without the availability of an objective account of goods and harm, there is then no complaint that K can make in this case. It is, of course, unfortunate if individuals should feel harmed at the way the world works, but if the harm is only a subjective harm, it makes no sense to complain to the world, in contrast to complaining to another agent in the case of intentional unfreedom. Therefore, if we are to acknowledge the idea of impersonal unfreedoms not only do we need an antecedent account of the good, but that account must deliver a notion of objective goods and harms.

3. Claims of needs

The above is very much a part of a general line of argument against liberalism that is common nowadays. This argument stresses the way that the liberal concentration on rights and other deontological concepts creates a moral vacuum in which the subject reduces to the vanishing point of the transcendental ego with no conception of the good to give substance to moral life.[1] It is a very persuasive line of argument. However, might the argument not be blocked by appeal to the concept of

[1] A good instance of this sort of argument can be found in Michael Sandel, *Liberalism and the Limits of Justice* (Cambridge 1982).

needs as employed in (4)? Perhaps – so the thought would go – the appeal to needs could establish the claims of unfreedom in a way that meets the above argument and without involving socialists in the admittedly difficult enterprise of providing a theory of the good, let alone a theory that accommodates the idea of there being such a thing as *the* good. I do not think the appeal to needs can work here, for much the same reason as the appeal to freedom was seen to fail.

When we talk of needs we have to distinguish between *conditional* and *unconditional*. Conditional needs (sometimes referred to as 'instrumental') are needs involved in claims like 'X needs 1500 more votes', 'X needs a new car', 'X and her family need a larger house'. Such claims of need are conditional upon some further desires of the claimant. They are claims of the general form,

(5) X needs N in order to F

Someone might need a new car if she is to take a touring holiday on the continent, or to keep up with some perceived image, but her need is not unconditional. Similarly, someone might need a new house if she is to be able to spread her family around the house in the manner she deems desirable, but this is hardly an unconditional need. Conditional needs are not always expressed in such a way as to make explicit the condition that grounds the needing. If so the claim is said to be elliptical.

On the other hand, it seems in order to admit a category of unconditional needs.[1] That is, there are claims of needs which not only are not expressed as conditional needs but are not elliptical for some such expression. That there are such needs is seen by the following consideration. If K says that she needs a new car we can reveal the elliptical nature of this by saying,

(6) You do not need the new car because you do not need the continental touring holiday.

---

[1] I am indebted to David Wiggins, *Needs, Values, Truth: essays in the philosophy of value* (Oxford 1987), from which I have benefited at this point. However, although I have borrowed some of his distinctions, I have rendered them in slightly different terminology and I am not as confident as he is of the fruitfulness of the concept of need.

But not only does this bring out the ellipsis in her claim, it brings out an unconditional need. The second occurrence of 'need' in (6) cannot be a conditional need. If that were the case, (6) would amount to no more than

(7) You do not need the new car because you do not need the continental touring holiday because you do not need the ... and so on.

Plainly, this is silly. *K*'s lack of a need for a continental touring holiday is a lack of an unconditional need. What we are saying when we respond with (6) is that the elliptical need claim is not grounded in something that *K* just plain needs unconditionally. The force of (6) is something like

(8) You do not need the new car because you will not be *fundamentally harmed* if you go without it.

Unconditional needs then are those needs such that, without their being granted, the agent would suffer fundamental harm. Short of being convinced of some fanciful story about how *K would* be fundamentally harmed if she did not get her continental touring holiday, we are licensed to observe that she does not need a new car because she does not unconditionally need the holiday.

There is then a viable distinction to be drawn between conditional and unconditional needs. Clearly the sorts of claims of needs that figure in (4) are unconditional needs. Why then will these not do in giving an account of the goods required to bolster the deontology of freedom and rights? The answer is simply that, as with the claims of freedom in §2, the claims of needs are not prior to our accounts of the good. The priority is the other way around. At best, giving voice to claims of needs is just to give voice to our conception of goods and harms. It is not an alternative to characterising goods and harms.

An unconditional need is one the absence of which creates a fundamental harm for the subject. But although such needs are unconditional, they are still *relative*. They are relative to one's conception of what constitutes a fundamental harm, one's conception of the good. Raymond Plant spoke of needs at a high level of generality: needs for 'health, physical integrity, education and a reasonable level of income.'[1] But of course, without some account of what *is* a reasonable level of income, and what level of education and health provision is required by these needs, such high-level claims are virtually uncontentious. Further, any account of what is deemed to be the appropriate level of satisfaction of these needs will, perforce, draw upon a conception of the good. It is *that* that provides content to the claims of needs. To put the point another way: If we work with claims of needs that are more specific – say, a claim that everyone has a right to full employment to satisfy the need of fulfilment and having a place in society – then, although we would have something that would probably sort out the socialists from the rest, we also have something the credibility of which is much harder to sustain. For such a need is relative to certain assumptions about the good. What is required is to show that these assumptions are legitimate, for they are contestable and, indeed, strongly contested. They are contested just because they are constitutive of a particular conception of the good life.

So although there are such things as unconditional needs, they are relative. They are relative to a conception of the good life. In that case the appeal to needs does nothing to settle the issue about the requirement for an account of the good. Put another way, if the appeal to fundamental needs here is legitimate, it can only be because we have shown how it is legitimate to invoke the concept of the good.

4. Interference and regulation

The above argument has been a negative one concerned with the inadequacies of recent attempts to write the theory of socialism without embracing the need to give a central role to the concept of the good life. It is now time to turn to the positive argument for the same conclusion.

As I have already noted, socialists typically feel entitled to interfere in social and economic life. But for such interference to be legitimate we must have a theoretical framework that invokes something more than the abstract claims of rights and

---

[1] In the *New Statesman*, March 1987, p. 14.

freedom so far considered. We need the availability of the concept of the good life. The centrality of this need can be argued for positively in the following way.

First we need to establish that this longing to interfere and regulate is a *bona fide* characteristic of socialism. That it is can be seen by considering the alternative. The alternative is this: we accept a laissez-faire free market in moral values. The alternative is deregulation of the moral market. This must be anathema to socialists, for such deregulation leads inevitably to that most extreme of liberal positions, the libertarianism that has, of late, informed so much of the policy initiatives experimented with upon British and US citizens. Such deregulation ignores the fact that not all capitalistic acts between consenting adults have beneficial consequences. As ever, it is the notion of the harmful consequences that often flow from such deregulation, whether in the economic or the moral sphere, that informs and justifies the desire to interfere and regulate. To take a simple example. Despite the bleating and passion that was aroused when compulsory seat-belt legislation was introduced in the UK, I suspect few now doubt that it was a good measure. And the important point is that it is the consequences for good or bad that justify that piece of interfering legislation.

Without some legitimacy for interference in social and economic life, the alternative amounts to no less than the libertarian free-marketeering currently in vogue among western right-wing governments. Further, the legitimacy of interference appears to derive from some notion of the good or bad consequences of interference and non-interference. The real issue now must be this: Is it necessary, in order to justify a richer model of society than the libertarian one, that we possess the concept of *the* good life? Could we not have a licence to interfere for what appear to be socialist ends without this much theoretical baggage? It is this question that stands in need of a good answer.

5. Interference and the good

Suppose we could do without the notion of the good life. Suppose, that is, that we accept the liberal model of society in which the determination of the good is left to freely choosing individuals constrained only not intentionally and directly to bring harm to others. In other words, suppose we try to build socialism without accepting what I have called the Good Principle. This, you will recall, ran as follows:

> *The Good Principle*: There is more to the achievement of the good life than the satisfaction of individuals' actual preferences.

In rejecting the Good Principle we try to justify interference in the economic and moral markets without the theoretical encumbrance of the need to justify our talk of the good life. We want to interfere and ameliorate the harmful consequences that frequently arise when the economy is left deregulated: for example, unemployment. Can we justify this interference without the Good Principle? If we can, socialism does not need the Good Principle. But I shall argue that we cannot justify the interference without the Good Principle.

The following is an affirmative answer to this problem that is often implicit in much political activity. It is a failure. The answer goes like this: it denies that there is any legitimation problem for interference because there is sufficient consensus within society for the promotion of those lines of interference we feel compelled to promote. If we look hard enough at the moral contours of civil society as we find it, we discover that the sorts of interference proposed do not conflict with the moral consensus. Let me call this answer to our question 'the sentimental response'. For the proposal is that by looking at the sentiments and moral feelings currently active within civil society we will find sufficient consensus to endorse interferences that override the libertarian free market.

At the time of writing[1] the sentimental response is much in vogue in the UK. As the National Health Service veers towards collapse we hear a lot of breast-beating and exhortation as a rallying call goes out to capture the so-called moral high ground from which we can agree that we are fine fellows bound by a common sentiment to provide a health-care service that caters for all. Similarly with the responses to the changes in the education system. To date, most spokesmen on the Left have done little more than act as cheer leaders whipping up

---

[1] Autumn 1988.

the sentiments and smugly nodding to one another: 'We care for the poor and disadvantaged, don't we?'

I think there are two broad reasons why this sort of response fails. The first is this. When politicians go to whip up the sentiments they are met with little more than a whimper. I simply do not believe that there really exists the sort of first-order consensus within civil society that can make the sentimental response work. And remember, the notion of 'work' here is not that of whether the sentimental response offers *practical* help. The issue is whether it offers theoretical legitimacy to interference. Our fundamental problem is the problem of legitimation. People often lament the passing of the post-war consensus and the way that Thatcherism has transcended it. I do not believe it was ever really there.[1] What was around, until the economic bubble was pricked by the successive oil crises of the seventies, was simply an enormous glut. We lived through a period of economic boom unparalleled in human history.[2] Admittedly, the boom occurred mainly within the western industrialised nations and did so largely at the expense of the developing Third World, but within those constraints there was an enormous creation of wealth. It was the background wealth in the economy which, for a brief time, permitted vaguely defined sentiments to latch on to small fragments of that wealth and deliver a modicum of redistribution. The thought then is this: Whatever consensus existed with regard to state provision for the disadvantaged, it was a side-effect of the enormous wealth creation that occurred through the 50s and 60s, rather than a deliberate and consciously sought-for plan derived from carefully thought out first-order imperatives.

This claim helps explain the point noted in the Introduction that the Left in the UK is as often thought of in terms of particular methods and institutions of social organisation as in the goals that such methods and institutions are aimed at. So, when one thinks of the British Labour party, one thinks of various institutions: the National Health Service, the nationalised industries, the TUC, a system of progressive taxation; one rarely thinks of the end-state the realisation of

[1] Hence there is nothing much for the Labour Listens campaign to listen to!
[2] See F. Green & B. Sutcliffe, *The Profit System: the economics of capitalism* (London 1987), 284ff for the details to substantiate this remark.

which requires these institutions and methods – if indeed it does require these institutions. The goals have been left hazily defined in terms of some vague sentimental concern to assist the disadvantaged, with the appeal for some level of redistribution left at the level of a supposedly obvious, but barely articulated, intuition. It is because of this that we now face the urgent need to articulate our goals if we are to legitimate interference.

Now it may be thought that I have been too harsh on the postwar consensus and the condition of civil society at present. But the second main reason why I think the sentimental response to the problem fails shows that it would not matter if I am mistaken. For the second failing with the sentimental response is this: No legitimate licence for interference can be sustained by the liberal model and its rejection of the Good Principle.

Our problem is this: Can we justify interference from within the liberal model in which the determination of goods is left to freely choosing individuals? Now perhaps, so the thought might go, this problem could be resolved thus: if the state does interfere, is it really doing anything other than advertising the wishes of the majority? Let us examine this a little further.

If the state merely promotes the good life as determined by the individual agents within the state, does it then challenge the underlying liberal model? There is, of course, in such a scenario plenty of scope for fun issues in political science on how to construct voting systems that pick out, by whatever criteria are deemed appropriate, those aspects of the good which the state can legitimately take from its members and promote on their behalf. But is there an issue of political theory about the legitimacy of the state's promotion of some good when that good has been selected by whatever voting system is employed? Of course there are theoretical, or philosophical, issues concerning the selection of the criteria for evaluating different voting systems, but these are secondary once we have decided that the only appropriate determination of the good is by individuals. All that is left is the construction of the appropriate matrixes for arriving at some notion of what goods we collectively want to promote.

However, the situation is not as simple as this. In not challenging the basic model which leaves the determination of the good at the atomic level, we have to accept the following point: The notion of the goods we collectively want to promote is a *fiction*. There is no collective that selects goods. Selection goes on only at the individual level. Any talk of collective promotion of goods is merely complicated shorthand for saying that these goods, determined by individuals, have been selected by welfare function *f* as the goods most likely to satisfy something like most of the people most of the time. That is why I say that it is a technical issue of political science rather than a theoretical issue of political philosophy. Indeed, given the well-known paradoxes of social choice theory, it is not simply a technical issue, but just as much a pragmatic one, since no procedure for deriving a collective ordering of preferences from individual preference orderings can satisfy conditions that look very minimal.[1]

Why then is the sentimental response not an option? The simple reason for the unavailability of this option for the socialist is this: we are back to the pure economism about values briefly noted above. Such a position cannot encompass talk of the good, but merely the goods currently desired. Therefore it lacks the resources to license socialist interference and, worse than that, as I argue in the next section, such economism about values can ultimately give no content to the idea of individual goods either. At this point all that is left for socialism is to identify itself with some array of first-order values and, having done so, to cross its fingers and hope enough people will find like-minded sentiments within their hearts to give it all a whirl. And apart from the fact that such compliant quietude offers little prospect of bringing in the New Jerusalem this side of eternity, it means that, in the end, socialism has nothing distinctive to offer that is not also found in liberalism. The only difference left to mark the distinction between a liberal and a socialist would be their differing propensities with regard to first-order value selections. In terms of the theoretical apparatus they bring to bear in their analyses of society there would be no difference at all.

It is here that we must make what will be, to some, a difficult choice. The first choice is the path of TB socialism which

---

[1] See I. McLean, *Public Choice: an introduction* (Oxford 1987), 165ff for an account of the various impossibility theorems in this area.

amounts to no more than a goody-goody version of liberalism. On this path lies nothing that cannot also be got within the framework of liberalism seasoned with a large sprinkling of egalitarian first-order principles. The cost of this option is the forfeit of any legitimacy to interfere with the workings of the free market either in the economic or the moral sphere, and the legitimacy of any critiques of the status quo. Down the second path lies the scope for a position in political philosophy worthy of distinction from liberalism. I call it socialism. Which path best fits the aspirations of those who, in the past, have taken this label is really of little consequence. With regard to the UK experience, I suspect too few are yet ready to choose the second path. I interpret that to mean that, as yet, there are few socialists in the UK. However, although this book is not intended as a systematic treatise on political philosophy, if the argument of the next section is right, the former of the two options just offered is incoherent. But this is not the place for such systematic canvassing of all available options. Here and now, the choice is between a version of liberalism and something that offers a theoretical alternative in our analysis of the ills of contemporary society.

I choose the latter option. This book is about the meaning of socialism, not a variant of liberalism. It may be that the position I develop cannot ultimately be sustained. If that is the case, there is no distinctive option in political philosophy for which we need trouble the English language for the name 'socialism'. However, I think that it is not the case. Choosing the former option we lose the normativity of the socialist position which envisages some end state of how things *ought* to be rather than as they actually *are*. On the former option what is *desirable* collapses into a function of what is *desired*. We then lose the distinctive idea of there being such a thing as the good life altogether. We lose the normative edge that comes from admitting the social dimension to the good life, the idea that socialism requires a good society and not just good individuals. This is the fundamental reason why socialism must reject the liberal model.

Society is more than the matrix of individuals pursuing their private conceptions of the good life. There is something that licenses the socialist interference, the intervention to regulate this matrix in the service of some end other than those of the individuals involved. Such an idea can be founded only upon a central role for the concept of the good life in socialist theory. There is such a thing as the good.

6. The paradox of the disappearing good

We might summarise the point of the last two sections abstractly, and in so doing I shall develop the argument from the claim that legitimate interference cannot be had on an individualist conception of goods to the claim that, given the liberal model, there is no concept of good at all. If that is right, then not only is the position that I am outlining coherent, but it has to be embraced as its opponent, liberalism, collapses. The point concerns the paradox of the disappearing good; it is, if you like, an extension of Sen's proof of the impossibility of a Paretian liberal.[1]

We assume the liberal model of society. That is to say, we assume that the determination of the good is the business of, and is only the business of, individual agents.[2] We can put this in terms of individual preference orderings. For some individual i, i's determination of the good amounts to some ordering of preferences $p(i)$. Each individual has an ordering of preferences, and the set of all such orderings $\{p(i_1) \dots p(i_n)\}$ is the data for our social choice theory. Now, on the liberal model there is no social dimension to the good. However, might we not amend that model by legitimating interference in terms of the good *as selected by a majority of the voters*, or whatever function of the voters you like? But for that to work we need some function $f\{p(i_1) \dots p(i_n)\}$ for deriving a social ordering P from all the individual orderings. Now, by Sen's theorem on the impossibility of deriving any social decision function from individual orderings, we know that no function exists that can be relied on to do this and satisfy certain minimal constraints. That means that there is no social ordering P which might be called the good life.

[1] A. Sen, 'The impossibility of a Paretian liberal', *Journal of Political Economy* 78 (1970), reprinted in his *Choice, Welfare and Measurement* (Oxford 1982).

[2] This is where we are considering something far more extensive than Sen. His impossibility result depends only on the assumption of *some* arena for sovereignty of an individual's preferences, not on the total determination of the good by the individual.

Now, if there is no such thing as the social ordering, the good life, there can be no such thing as the good that it is legitimate to promote by interference. For suppose we have some particular good x that occurs as one of the goods within the overall range ordered in the individuals' sets of preferences $p(i_1) \ldots p(i_n)$. Now suppose that among a certain proportion of the population x comes out on top of each of the preference orderings for these individuals. Whatever proportion these individuals may be of the total population, the *legitimacy* of the state's promotion of x is no more than the legitimacy of these individuals acting as a group to promote x. On the liberal model, it cannot be legitimate to promote some conception of the good just because you find yourself in the happy circumstance of being among a number of like-minded people. That alone cannot make it legitimate for you to act as a homogeneous unit and promote your ordering over others. But then nor can the state do this. Of course this is not to deny that in order to live in a highly complex integrated society like our own we need, for practical purposes, to solve all sorts of coordination problems. It is only to deny that there is any legitimacy to whatever coordination method is adopted given the liberal model. Far better then to keep the solution of our coordination problems as neutral as possible with regard to the good. In terms of state apparatus, far better then to have a guarantor state, not a managerial state – one that guarantees the minimalist deontology of libertarianism rather than one that manages the good life.

Another way of putting this is to say that there is no social dimension to the good life. That is why there are no standards of legitimacy with regard to the state promotion of this or that good, for there are no standards of social ordering. But that should have been obvious anyway given the liberal model which restricts the determination of the good life to the atomic level. The point is that within the individual's ordering task, she is constrained by principles of rationality, such as: Render all your preferences compatible. An agent cannot with just the same intensity of preference desire to do F and do G where doing the latter rules out the chance of doing the former. A difference of intensity of preference seems to be a requirement of rationality here. But that is precisely what is missing at the societal level in the liberal model and why there is no social dimension to the good life. For there is no way for the liberal to say it is *irrational* for one agent to desire to do *F* and another to do *G* with the same intensity. That is just the standard coordination problem for democrats. That the good life has no social dimension is why the concept of democracy is such an issue given the liberal model. And democracy usually is given the liberal model.

But matters are worse for the liberal. If there is no social dimension to the good life, there can be no individual dimension either, unless one thinks that we can derive substantive moral imperatives from pure rationality alone. And down that path lie the wrecks of innumerable Kantian projects in ethics. All this, of course, is just another way of approaching the argument about the threat, under liberalism, of the moral agent disappearing down the vanishing plughole of the transcendental ego.[1] The point is that the assumption of the liberal model denies a social dimension to the good life. *There are no normative bonds to bind individuals together. The only bonds are those shifting contracts struck in a moral vacuum.* Given the atomistic starting point there is no way to reconstruct something that might be called the good life; that is, there is no way to reconstruct the normativity of moral values. And now, further, the normativity cannot be reconstructed at the atomic level. For although the individual agent will be constrained by principles of formal rationality, such as:

Do not concurrently desire *F* and *G* with the same intensity where one precludes the other.

There is nothing within formal rationality to stop our desiring both at different times. The individual's moral life extends no further than the boundaries of the specious here and now. I cannot rationally chose to do *F* now and *G* now. But rationality does not restrict my choosing *F* over *G* now, and *vice versa* tomorrow. The atomism here is the same as that which enabled Hume to observe that rationality was indifferent to the choice between the destruction of the whole world and the scratching of his little finger. And just as Hume's atomism left no place for

[1] See Sandel, op. cit., for such an argument.

normativity within the moral and causal realms, so too, on the liberal model, all normativity vanishes.

The reason that the normativity of values collapses under liberalism is connected with very general issues about the grounds of normativity. Any account of our moral values must capture the normativity of values. That is, any account must capture the fact that our moral values *impel* us to act in various ways. Indifference is not an option in our response to situations of moral significance. It is simply the hallmark of moral irrelevance. But for our moral values to have the power to compel action the ground of the normativity must transcend the individual agent. The reason is not epistemological. It is not that if we ground the power of values in the individual it leaves the normativity too fickle. The reason is more substantive, it is that unless the ground of moral powers transcends the individual, no content can be given to the normativity of the values. For suppose that the normativity consisted in the agent's decision to count, for example, kind actions as good. The agent is then creating the *rule* that kind actions are good. But if that rule is to have the power of normativity we associate with moral values, it must have a generality of application. That is, in saying of an action x_1 that it is kind an agent is committed to saying that actions $x_2 \ldots x_n$, of a sort with x_1 are also kind. The normativity of values consists in the normativity of this commitment. What this amounts to is the idea that in saying of the first action that it was kind the agent must have *meant* that actions relevantly similar would also be kind. In calling x_1 kind the agent submits herself to a rule which determines that the relevantly similar actions are also kind. And it must be an act of submission here, not creation.

Submission is the only appropriate way of describing the rule. Otherwise the normativity vanishes. For suppose the agent determines that x_1 is kind by an act of individual choice. If that is the ground of the value, there is now nothing to determine which rule the agent has submitted to. For whatever future actions $x_2 \ldots x_n$ that may be witnessed, the agent will be free to 'bend' the rule in whatever way she desires. The problem here is not a moral one about the agent's sincerity in submitting to a rule. The problem is about the coherence of there being such a thing as a rule if the ground of the rule has to be fixed in the individual choice. For suppose that x_1 is an action of helping a disabled person across a busy road. In calling the action kind surely the agent has committed herself to count all helpings of disabled persons across busy roads kind? But this is not so. For example, it is not kind to help disabled persons across busy roads when they do not want to cross the road. Well, perhaps that is obvious and in making the original ascription of kindness she *meant* only to count cases where the person wanted to cross the road. But if the agent did not say that, or think it, how did she mean it unless we take her to be submitting to a rule that imposes upon her rather than one of her own creation. Worse than that, there is an infinite number of possible exceptions and qualifications to the situation of disabled persons before a busy road, and it is impossible to have all these before one's mind in formulating the rule, choosing the value, when saying that x_1 is kind. But in that case, if the value resides in the individual agent's choice, no rule can be fixed. No normativity can be constructed from such a meagre atomistic starting point. An infinite number of possible continuations of the rule are left open by the initial ascription of kindness, but in that case no rule whatsoever has been fixed. The way out of this problem is not to give up on the normativity of rules, it is simply to acknowledge that their normativity comes from without. Moral norms are an imposition, not a creation.[1]

What has gone wrong here is this. We have been looking in the wrong place to found the good life (the normativity of values) and a truly civil society. It is not enough to expect to find a truly socialist civil society by looking simply at what agents *actually* desire and, adopting the sentimental response, hoping to employ the state to interfere and promote what is desired. That loses the normative edge that makes us socialists in the first place: the normative edge that gives us the notion that there is a way society ought to be, regardless of how people evaluate the way it actually is. I shall now argue that we can only provide a distinctive notion of what socialism is by rejecting the prevailing assumptions of liberal theory. We need to examine the conditions necessary for the good life, for a truly

---

[1] The above argument draws upon Wittgenstein's account of rule following. For more on this, see my 'The transcendental grounds of meaning' in *Scepticism and Meaning*, ed. K. Puhl (Berlin & New York, forthcoming).

civil society. At the same time, I shall be rejecting TB socialism, the thesis that socialism is to be identified with specific first-order imperatives. Rather I shall be pursuing an identification of socialism as a *second-order* theory, a theory about the transcendental grounds of the good life – the conditions necessary for civil society.

7. Traditions, reference groups and the good life

Now, if the argument of the last section is right, we cannot hope to rebuild the normativity of the good life. We cannot construct a truly civil society, if we start with the liberal model. But we need this normativity if we are to answer the fundamental problem of legitimation. The sentimental response is unavailable, for (a) the consensus simply is not there, and (b) even if it were, from within the liberal model there is no such thing as the good life. At the very best there is simply a fortuitous and perhaps temporary solution to our coordination problems. We must start instead with moral life as we find it in our experience and see what is constitutive of it. In doing this I shall give a preliminary statement of the main critique of capitalism that I shall develop in the next chapter.

It seems an undeniable and wholly understandable fact about our moral lives that our concern for others is sensitive to distance, both spatial and temporal. That is to say, we find it easier to have a moral concern for those of our immediate family, work colleagues, fellow members of sports and social clubs, social and economic classes, etc. We capture this fact by saying that our moral concerns are mediated by the *reference groups* we share with those who are the objects of our concern.[1] For example, the nearest and most important reference group is the family. The idea of the reference group is important for my development of socialism.

I shall employ Runciman's notion of a *reference group*, but I want to modify the concept by broadening its application.

---

[1] I take the terminology of 'reference groups' from Runciman: see his *Relative Deprivation and Social Welfare* (London 1970). However, Runciman used the notion to capture the way in which claims of welfare deprivation were always made relative to a reference group which was socially close to the claimant. I shall be employing the concept in a slightly broader way; see below.

Ryan,[1] in a discussion that neatly captures the limitations of our moral concerns, observes that what engages the moral concern of most people is largely domestic matters. It is understandable that we should find it easier and more compelling to have moral concern for those of our own family, neighbours and colleagues. We know all too well the difficulty of feeling the same intensity of concern for those in distant places (and times) until some striking image or news bulletin 'brings it all home'. However we may judge this differential response to others, it is hard to see it as other than inevitable.

I shall speak then of reference groups as the means through which we learn and in which we ground our moral traditions. That is, the concept serves both to demarcate those communities from which we learn our moral norms. Also, it provides the means through which our moral concerns are realised. Each of us inhabits a variety of roles in our social life, roles which bring with them different codes of conduct some of which contribute to our moral code. I am not only a father and husband, with all the requirements and privileges that that involves, but a member of a college, an employee of a university, a member of a political party, etc. I might become an activist in some pressure group, or join some recreational club, and each time I take on such a further role further reference groups are taken on as a ground for the rules by which I live, some of which are moral rules. Our nearest, and arguably most important, reference group is the family. It is here that we first learn the moral traditions that guide us through later life. Other obvious but broader reference groups are the church, the factory, the social club, the neighbourhood, etc. The reference group then serves a dual role, that of (i) a grounding for our moral traditions, and (ii) the arena in which we employ our moral concern.[2]

The reference groups which we acknowledge provide the currency for the employment of our moral traditions.[3] In order to feel concern for others we have to see them as like ourselves,

---

[1] See A. Ryan, *Property and Political Theory* (Oxford 1984) and his example, p. 179: 'Three men digging in the same hole to locate water, gas and electricity mains will be acutely aware of differentials in their pay; about the wealth of Lord Cowdray they neither know nor care.'

[2] (ii) is the concept Runciman employed.

[3] I use the word 'tradition' deliberately. It is *not* the private property of the Right when speaking of moral traditions.

to bring them within some reference group within which we act out our daily dramas. Normally it is not enough just to know that another is simply a fellow human being. We can be told time and time again that fellow humans are suffering from famine in East Africa, but what finally plucks the moral chords is not this sharing of the most abstract reference group, but rather the closer images that reveal *families, mothers and children, husbands and wives* huddled together in a shared recognisable bond of human love and suffering. When we see the father and mother weep over the emaciated corpse of a young child, we fall susceptible to the sentiment 'There but for the grace of God ...'

In claiming that our concern for others requires the common currency of some relatively close reference group (think how difficult it would be to feel moral concern for alien life-forms which looked like battered carpet slippers!) I do not mean to be making a normative claim. It is simply that that is how things are. It was not, I think, always so. Our ability to feel concern for others was not always as described in the last paragraph. It is not that I think that there was a time when we did not need to employ a shared reference group as currency of concern. Rather I think that there may have been a time when an abstract universal reference group had bite. That is to say, there was a time when it was enough, I hazard to suppose, to know that another was a soul in the eyes of God for the other to be an object of our concern. The reference group formed of the creations of the Almighty was a reference group that had bite. It played a substantial role in determining the contours of our moral life. In just the sense that such a reference group fails to bite now, it is fair to say that we live in a secular age however much religious activity may be witnessed at any particular place or time. The modern predicament is very much that of learning to live in a God-less world, a world where the cosmic glue that held our moral concerns together in the all encompassing reference group of God's creation has lost its pull. Of course this is not to deny that, even when things were different, plenty of moral and political disagreement was possible and did occur. The point is simply this. There was available a way of life, a way of thinking and feeling, that could be employed to work through disagreements. In contrast, in the modern world, the problem seems often to be that we do not even know how to begin thinking, talking and feeling our way around the political dilemmas that confront us.[1]

MacIntyre has written provocatively of the demise of the virtues and the breakdown of moral life.[2] I have much sympathy with his account and take the picture he presents of the modern world to be explained by this removal of an all-encompassing reference group for our moral traditions.

Let us then not ignore the particularity of our moral lives, the requirement, in expressing a moral concern for others, that we see them as co-members of some reference group. It is the sharing of reference groups which provides the contours to our moral lives: why we help some and not others. Now it may well be the case that there was a time when there existed a universal reference group that successfully impinged upon us. If that, or something approximating to it, was once the case, it no longer is. But we need not despair at its demise. Let us note rather what seems to be required, in the absence of such a transcendent reference group, for the good life to proceed. What seems to be required is something like this. We need to be able to fashion mechanisms, ways of thinking and feeling, that will enable us to extend our reference groups where required, and to overcome those clashes which arise when the products of our reference groups conflict; that is, in situations where your reference group and the norms it supplies you with conflict with my reference group and the norms I derive from it. Whenever the traditions learnt from our various reference groups conflict, the requirement of the moral life, the requirement of the idea that there is such a thing as *the* good life, demands that we find some way to repair that rent in the moral fabric of our community. In such circumstances we need to construct new traditions of thought and feeling to enable the continuation of the good life and the construction of new reference groups to sound out the contours of a new moral experience.

The requirement of shared reference groups fuels a conception of the good life. It can only sustain it if our

---

[1] It is no accident that I speak of ways of 'thinking, talking and feeling'. The notion of a tradition that I am invoking is *not* simply that of a particular *language* or theory, it is a way of living. As such it is not something discovered by simple armchair reflection.

[2] A. MacIntyre, *After Virtue* (London 1981).

traditions have the resources to pursue disagreements to a resolution by the creation of new and extended reference groups. There needs to be a practice of reflection that enables critique of traditions. Such a practice will, most likely, have a central role for a critical concept of ideology to be employed in jettisoning traditions. I shall develop such a concept in Chapter 3. The two things, the need for the reference groups and the demand that they be susceptible to a charge of ideology in situations of conflict, go hand-in-hand.

8. Capitalism and the disruption of traditions

The requirement that our reference groups be extendable to overcome conflict is a demand derived from the theory of ideology. It is required in order that we strive to construct a non-ideological tradition of the good life. And central here is the thought that it is capitalism itself which stands in the way of such a construction. There are two claims I would be willing to defend at this point, a historical claim about the fragmentation of our moral traditions and a conceptual point about the way in which capitalism hinders the rebuilding of our moral traditions. I shall introduce the claim here before arguing for it in the next chapter, where I shall also offer a precise definition of capitalism. The conceptual claim is the central one for the purposes of my argument, but I shall sketch the historical point first, although nothing that follows hinges on its correctness.

The historical point is the claim that it was the emergence of capitalism that brought about the fragmentation of our reference groups and the dissolution of the normativity of the good. The idea is simply this. It was only by virtue of the dissolution of the weave of reference groups, the dissolution of the good life, that capitalism could flourish. For what capitalism requires is the 'freeing' of the labouring subject from the norms of, for example, feudalism, which bound him to the land and the master, so that he could enter 'free' contracts for his labour power.[1] The emergence of the market in labour

---

[1] For an excellent analysis of the labour market which stresses the differences between this 'market' and conventional commodity markets, see Claus Offe, *Disorganized Capitalism* (Oxford 1986), esp. chs. 1 & 2. As Offe notes, 'The recruitment of labour power is supposed to depend upon "free

power required the dissolution of the reference groups, so that one subject came to face another no longer within the web of norms presented by the sharing of various reference groups. Instead one subject came to face another solely as competitor in the market to supply Capital with the labour power necessary for the maximisation of profit. Capital needs labour power to be freed from the normative bonds of our moral traditions, or else its supply will be economically inefficient. And of course, for Capital, the only measure of the adequacy of its supply is the economic efficiency in terms of profit maximisation.

Whether or not this historical claim can be made good, it is not necessary to the argument which follows. What is necessary is this idea: Capitalism prevents the rebuilding of the traditions of thought and feeling that would enable us to construct the reference groups necessary to see our way through the political dilemmas of the modern world. Capitalism cannot abide the construction of relationships other than those economic ones in which it places one labourer in relation with another. As soon as labourers construct relationships other than that of competitors in the labour market, the accumulation of capital decreases.[1] It is a necessary part of the capital/labour relationship that Capital should continually seek to achieve ever cheaper and more productive supplies of labour. For as soon as one capital plant achieves such a supply, the rest must follow on pain of going out of business. It is this total economisation of human relationships under capitalism that stands in the way of the repair to the good life and is at the basis of the development of socialism that I have to offer. For capitalism to flourish, moral agency has to be replaced by economic agency, and therefore it is no good trying to put a 'human' face upon capitalism. As long as the underlying economic arrangement is a capitalist one,

---

choice" and is, therefore, not restricted by normative obligations of assistance on the feudal ties of labour to the land.' But aside from Offe's point that it turns out not be real 'free' choice, the more fundamental question is why it should be thought better to chose one's labouring role in the moral vacuum of individualistic liberalism than within the normative traditions of reference groups that can be shown non-ideological? Of course, this is *not* to suppose that the normative traditions of feudalism were ever so.

[1] For example, the unionisation of Labour can be seen as the construction of just such reference groups anathema to Capital's pursuit of profit.

there is no room for the construction of the reference groups required to make that face more than a shallow mask.

It is the fragmentation of the reference groups grounding our moral traditions that characterises the modern world and the spirit of *anomie* prevalent. For a return to the virtues, I do not think we need to return to a way of life where a universal religiously defined reference group takes hold of our lives. Indeed I do not see how we could return to such a way. Reference groups cannot be imposed at will. The demise of the religious way of life and the concomitant fragmentation of the moral life that came about with secularisation is irreversible. What is needed is a framework in terms of which we may weave together our reference groups. What is needed is that the activity of discovering shared reference groups be allowed to proceed unhindered. The programme is not a Kantian-inspired top-down activity in which we start with an abstract universal reference group – the kingdom of ends – with which we try to encompass all moral life. Rather we start from the bottom, from the contours of our everyday moral dramas, and seek to broaden these to provide reference groups that are alive, full of the breath of daily moral life. The task is not to construct an overall reference group, but simply to get our particular reference groups working in unison. And here is the cornerstone of the modern predicament. It is not just the fragmentation of moral life with the diversification of reference groups brought on by secularisation that is our problem: a diversification which, taken to its extreme, results in the individual of classical liberal theory. The reference group is *me*![1] Our problem lies in the factors which inhibit the repair of the fragmentation. The suggestion is that the chief factor involved is capitalism. Capitalism requires, and receives, the economisation of all social relationships in place of the normal sharing of reference groups which alone ensure the continuation of the moral life.

Many people are keen to extol the virtues of community solidarity. This has long been central to much Left-wing politics in the UK. At the same time there is, frankly, much that is embarrassing about the virtues we find in many

---

[1] Recall the observation made in the Introduction about how we can measure the demise of the good life by the preponderance of claims of rights and the current advance of such claims with the case of children's rights.

traditional white, male-dominated working-class communities, to say nothing of the unions. However, what is important about the notion of the community is that *it is the repository of the good life*. Whatever qualms we may have about some of the values manifested within the communities cherished by the Left, we cannot and should not have any qualms about the existence of such reference groups. The importance of the notion of community solidarity is this: It is the community which supports the traditions of thought and feeling that are required in order to sustain a compelling moral concern for others. Whatever particular values may have figured (and perhaps in places still do) in the traditional communities of British working-class life, the importance of the community lay in the way it provided a framework through which the life of another could, quite naturally and unreflectively, become an object of concern. And whatever you think about the particular values embodied in such traditions, the demise of such modes of living is the greatest tragedy of the modern predicament.

2

Ownership, Capital and the Economy

1. Introduction

Socialism is usually characterised by a demand for the social
ownership of the means of production. In contrast, I have
argued that its central characteristic is a concern for the good
life: furthermore, a concern that can only be realised by
acknowledging the social foundation of our conceptions of the
good. What then, if any, is the connection between questions
about the ownership of capital and my account of socialism?
This is the question I shall answer in this chapter. In doing so I
shall elaborate the critique of capitalism proposed in §8 of the
last chapter.

My main claim will be this: *Ownership* of capital is not, in
itself, what matters. What matters is whether the economy is
so organised that the needs of people and the authority of the
good are displaced by the needs of Capital and the profit
motive. And although certain patterns of ownership may be
more conducive to propounding the needs of Capital, and some
patterns more conducive to defending the authority of the
good, there is no straightforward connection between the two
spheres. If this is right, it provides one explanation why the
UK experience of nationalisation has been such an irrelevance
and disaster. First, I clarify the definition of capitalism and
explore the territory of claims that private ownership of capital
is a Bad Thing.

2. What is capitalism, and who is a capitalist?

So far I have used the term 'capitalism' without attempting to
be precise about what it means. Given that I shall now
elaborate the idea that the problem of capitalism is *not* the

private ownership of the means of production, I must say exactly what I mean by the word. Most people identify capitalism as the private ownership of capital and so the intelligibility of my argument requires a precise alternative definition.

What I mean by capitalism is this:

(1) A capitalist society is one in which the economy is primarily arranged for the benefit of Capital.

Note, despite the break with orthodox usage, that this can easily be confused with a usage which identifies capitalism as a society in which the means of production is owned privately. The reason is that (1) is easily confused with

(2) A capitalist society is one in which the economy is primarily arranged for the benefit of capitalists.

But (1) and (2) become equivalent only if we assume that the interests of Capital are identical with the interests of capitalists, and there is no reason to make that identification. (1) is a *structural* definition of capitalism. It defines capitalism in terms of the way that society is organised by abstract economic requirements. (2) personifies these requirements in the interests of a particular class of people, those who own capital. This personification may not have mattered if the ownership of capital still fitted the classical pattern of nineteenth-century capitalism. But that pattern is long since altered (I shall trace some of the consequences of these changes below). However, even if in the last century the interests of capital coincided with the interests of capitalists, that was no more than a coincidence. With regard to the theoretical interest in capital from the point of view of socialism, the overriding importance has always been the arrangement of the economy as characterised by (1), not by (2).

Complementary to the above definition of capitalism, we might also provide a more specific definition of a capitalist. Now clearly in so far as one is an owner of capital one is thereby a capitalist. That is uncontroversial but, of itself, of little interest or significance. This is borne out by the vacuity of the thought[1] that, by diversifying share ownership and home ownership through society, the UK has been turned into a nation of capitalists and the brain death of socialism has been assured. For although such broadening of capital ownership makes more people capitalists in the literal sense of possession of fragments of capital, it does not make us all capitalists in the following theoretically more interesting sense:

(3) A capitalist is one who is committed to pursuing the interests of capital before the interests of people.

As the primary interest of Capital is the raising of, and the potential to raise, profits, the theoretically interesting notion of a capitalist is that of someone for whom the profit motive and its accessory, the mechanism of the free market, is the principal means of organising society for the distribution of goods and services. (3) then comes to this:

(4) A capitalist is one who believes that the free market, driven by the profit motive, is the most appropriate way of organising the distribution of goods and services in society.

And it is (4) that I shall appeal to from now on when I speak of capitalists, just as it is (1) that I shall appeal to when I speak of capitalism.

Note this: if these definitions can be sustained, they are of enormous practical, as well as theoretical benefit. In the UK a great deal of the loss of a sense of direction on the Left has been due to the way that the Right has, without opposition, laid down the agenda for discussion, often steamrolling allegiances where none should be apparent. For example, in the UK the owners of small businesses are automatically assumed by all parties, including themselves, to have natural alliances with the Conservative government. But this is folly, although, cramped within historically persuasive cultural class loyalties, it is, perhaps, not surprising. Consider this. Although the owners of small businesses own capital, it does not follow from that that they are capitalists (in the sense of (4)). Indeed, often

---

[1] Due to Mrs Thatcher.

enough, they are far from it. The unfettered pursuit of the profit motive, as embodied in the deregulation of the financial markets of the City of London has, for many small businesses, spelled outright disaster. The average small business, as much as the individual citizen, needs a breathing space within the hurly-burly of the free market. The inability of the Left to recognise the potential for alliances with those who happen to own some capital, although perhaps unsurprising, has been historically important in the continuing ineffectual opposition to a govern-ment riding high on naïve notions of where its natural consti-tuency lies. As indicated, I am sure that much of the Left's short-sightedness here is due to historical and cultural hosti-lities within the straightjacket of the English class system. And although there have been models to appeal to for the English Left, the Italian and French Left, for example have not been so restricted in their choice of allies against Capital. Nevertheless I do not think that these cases arose from considered theoretical reflection, but more by the same historical and cultural forces that, in the UK, have produced such stultifying results.

But before we get carried away in by these definitions to fashion prescriptions for our current problems, we must see if they are theoretically viable, and whether the alternative literal accounts of capitalism and questions of ownership can still deliver any use. I turn now, therefore, to consider why the identification of socialism with an issue about ownership fails.

3. Some problems with ownership

Socialism has usually been thought to hold that private ownership of capital is, in some way, responsible for the ills of contemporary society. I think this is mistaken, but it is sufficiently close to the truth for it to be instructive to see where and how it is mistaken. We shall have to make a detour to consider the charges of exploitation and alienation made against capitalist society and, eventually, to give an account of these charges that can be made to stick. I start with more familiar, although erroneous, beliefs about ownership.

Too often people are attracted to socialism as a result of a nebulous belief that, in some unspecified way, capitalism fails to provide for a fair distribution of property and wealth. But even if that feeling were articulated and substantiated, all sorts of remedies are possible to amend the distribution problems. Are we socialists if we favour state ownership of the means of production? And what about worker-ownership in, for example, workers' collectives? Or again, what about punitive taxes raised on the owners of capital? Historically the former has been most prevalent among those who call themselves socialists, not only in the state socialisms of Eastern Europe but in the thinking behind the demand for nationalisation of large companies and banks which, until recently, figured large in the British Labour Party.[1] It should not have required the experience of repression that has occurred in many East European countries to realise that state ownership of the means of production is not the general panacea so often claimed.

If there were a reason for redistributing private ownership in favour of some form of social ownership of the means of production, great care would be needed in drawing the connection between ownership and the thwarting of socialist ideals. Otherwise we would risk using 'socialism' to mean little more that a system of social organisation in which everybody has a good time!

There are several problems which militate against an easy identification of the private ownership of capital and some readily perceived evil in contemporary society, whether that is expressed in terms of alienation or exploitation. I shall list these problems here so that, by comparison, the nature of the analysis to be offered may be more readily seen. The problems I have in mind are these:

(i) Is it plausible to blame the private ownership of capital with exploitation and inequality?

(ii) If there is exploitation, can this not be remedied by taxation, as under contemporary welfare state capitalism?

(iii) Is ownership really so important? In a modern limited liability company it is the managers who confront the workers, not the owners.

[1] For example, see Cripps et al., *Manifesto* (London 1979).

(iv) Even if private ownership were abolished, would it not be the case that someone would have to assume the power and control of the classical capitalist?

(v) Can central state planning adequately replace the efficiency of the market for maintaining industry and commerce?

These five issues are all large, complicated and live contemporary topics. Together they indicate a muddled morass of problems confronting the socialist who believes in the abolition of private property. I shall comment briefly on each issue in turn before turning to consider the reasons for thinking that what is wrong with capitalism is not the pattern of ownership rights. Once we get that matter right issues (i) – (v) will take care of themselves.

(i) The experience of those who have lived through some of the most repressive regimes in human history is testimony to the idea that simple greed, envy and exploitation can thrive just as readily in a state-run economy with state ownership of capital as in a free-market economy where capital is privately owned. Any defence of socialism must acknowledge that and provide an analysis of the issue about ownership that accommodates recent history.

(ii) The concept of exploitation is usually understood in the framework of Marx's labour theory of value and the theory of surplus value.[1] According to this all value is a function of the labouring process. More precisely, the value of a commodity is a function of the amount of labour time that would be needed to replace it.[2] However, the worker does not receive the full product of her labour. Instead she receives just enough to

[1] Allen Wood, *Karl Marx* (London & Boston 1981) is a good source for an account of these theories; but see also Gerry Cohen's exemplary 'The labour theory of value and the concept of exploitation', *Philosophy & Public Affairs* (1979), reprinted in *Marx, Justice and History* (Princeton 1980), for an analysis of the failure of the labour theory of value to sustain charges of exploitation. I am much indebted to Cohen's essay.

[2] This is in contrast to the muddled idea that the value of a commodity is something *created* by the labouring process and, as it were, cemented into the commodity at the point of creation by the labourer. On this see Cohen, op. cit.

sustain herself, and her class, for the activity of labouring. The rest of the product of the labour, the value of the commodity, is taken by the capitalist. It is in this that the worker is exploited as the capitalist lives off the value which would not have been created without the work of the labourer. There are innumerable problems with this idea of exploitation.

First, as Marx clarified the issue in the *Critique of the Gotha Programme*, the worker is not entitled to the full product of her labour, because of the need for those items which we might cluster under the heading re-investment. This will include safeguards against risk, literal reinvestment in plant necessary to continue and develop the manufacturing process, collective consumption (health care, etc.), and so on. Therefore, of the value V of a commodity, V minus wages W does not represent the surplus taken by the capitalist. Rather, it is $V-(W+E)$, 'E' for acceptable necessary expenditure under reinvestment. Call $V-(W+E)$ the surplus S that accrues to the capitalist. Now we can ask all sorts of questions about S.

First, is S a significant proportion of the gross value V? It might turn out that the surplus left for the capitalist is proportionately so small that, even if it were thought that it warranted the label of 'exploited value', its redistribution through the workforce would result in a negligible increase in income.

Secondly, suppose S is a significant proportion of V by whatever criterion of significance you like, why could it not be redistributed through a system of progressive taxation much as exists, to some degree or another, in the systems of welfare state capitalism found in the western democracies.[1]

Thirdly, even if S were a significant proportion of V, before we apply any system of progressive taxation should we not allow for entrepreneurial skill? If so, that skill requires a return for contributing labour in the creation of V. Once we accept the need to acknowledge entrepreneurial skill as a factor in the labouring process creating the value, that labour needs to be recompensed to a degree to ensure its continued

---

[1] Of course, there is no shortage of conservative thinkers to say that S should not be redistributed so because it destroys business incentives, but I am asking the question for the socialist, not her opponent. For a particularly shrill statement of the opposing 'supply-side' view, cf. G. Gilder, *Wealth and Poverty* (New York 1981).

deployment. It may well be that, because of the risks involved, entrepreneurial skills require a greater reward than brute labour in order to encourage initiative and business acumen.

These three issues look to turn the labour theory of value into a double-edged weapon. They suggest ways in which the claim of exploitation is undermined rather than supported by the theory. However, although the three points raised here are familiar, and the sorts of issues frequently addressed in contemporary political debate, they altogether miss the point about the labour theory of value and the concept of exploitation.

The raising of these three points is generally fuelled by the notions of fairness and equality. This is explicit in the second point, where there is an assumption that the distribution of goods in society beyond the bare necessities should be an equal distribution. This is doubtless an important idea within the socialist panoply of ideals, but its appearance here, in arguing for a system of progressive taxation, is significant. After all, although it may be that a demand for simple equality is coherent and legitimate, at present we are trying to consider arguments connecting socialism with an attack on the private ownership of capital. But if our goal could be met simply by introducing an effective system of progressive taxation, privacy of ownership could hardly matter. It would then be the abstract demand for equality which did all the work, and if everyone had an equal share of goods why worry about the issue of ownership? It is important that we get clear just which assumption is doing what work in our theorising. Too often socialists move from discussing private ownership as the root of all evil to inequality as the culprit, without saying what the connection is. I shall discuss the more abstract question of the role of the concept of equality in socialism in Chapter 5. For the moment I want to clarify the role of ownership relations to political theory.

The reason why the issues about progressive taxation miss the fundamental point about property is this. For sure, entrepreneurial skill needs to be rewarded. But entrepreneurs are not necessarily the owners of capital. Entrepreneurs and their reward should be accounted for under W or, if you want to stress a difference in their work from that of the shop-floor worker, under E for necessary expenditure on reinvestment, etc. Either way, the reward due to entrepreneurs is accounted for in the proportion of the total value represented by ($W+E$). That still leaves the value $V-(W+E)$, which accrues to the capitalist *solely in virtue of her ownership of the capital and not in virtue of any work done*. That is the salient point about ownership. If you own capital you receive a share of the total value created by labour without doing any labour. The labour of the entrepreneur is irrelevant in all this. Also irrelevant are the questions about progressive taxation as long as these are confined to taxation on earned incomes. The issue about property is an issue about *unearned* income. And it is not an issue about the fairness of deriving an income from ownership, the salient point is simply the observation that ownership alone, without labour, grants the owner an income in contrast to all other groups in society.

So important is it to keep this point in mind that it is worth emphasising and noting as a special thesis:

> *The salient thesis about ownership*: Those who own capital receive an income for no reason other than that they own capital. (They may also receive an income in reward for entrepreneurial/manual skills if they are managers/workers as well as capitalists.)

For the moment, I make no claims about what follows from this point. Some may think that this feature of the private ownership of capital affronts some moral principle of fairness, but given the way in which I have said that I am developing the socialist position I do not wish to pursue that idea myself.

For Marx, the importance of the above thesis lay in the way it ensured class divisions in society which would, he thought, give rise to such contradictory impulses that a revolution would wipe out the divisions to produce a classless society. Note that this leaves Marx's point unconcerned with a moral denunciation of capitalism and capitalist distributions. For Marx, the point about ownership is that it fuels the contradictions that, in turn, fuel the dynamic of the materialist theory of history.[1] However, there is still an indirect need for a

---

[1] It is on this point, whether Marx had, or needed, a moral critique of capitalism, that much recent debate has centred. I follow Wood, op. cit., in thinking that Marx's point was independent on any moral disquiet he may

moral critique within Marx's theory. For although the central point about ownership is employed only to mark the class divisions in capitalist society, for those divisions to engender contradictions sufficient to require a communist revolution to overcome them, the working class will have to feel a strong moral antithesis to the capitalists. Without *that* the class divisions will fail to give rise to revolutionary activity, for if the workers are well rewarded for their skills, it is not at all clear that they will mind the point noted above as the salient thesis about ownership.[1]

(iii) As is often pointed out,[2] few companies today conform to the classical picture of capitalistic enterprise where the workers stand confronted with the owner and her family. With the development of the modern limited liability company ownership is diversified through the shareholders and it is the management and the board of directors who confront the workers. Given this, why should the question of ownership be so politically sensitive? For the power that controls the lives of the workforce and which traditionally resided directly in the capitalist is now to be found in the employees of the owners, although they are of course, subject to removal by the shareholders. This point reinforces the salient thesis isolated above. Whatever moral outrage socialists may have at the unequal distribution of labour, reward and benefits among workers and management, this can have nothing to do with the issue of the ownership of capital.

It is worth noting that this common point about the change of ownership patterns in modern business is now dated. Recent research suggests a slightly different picture.[3] Scott claims that the form of ownership which is replacing the old-style family firm is not the managerial enterprise of liberal theory

---

have had for capitalist property relations. On Marx's theory of history, see G.A. Cohen, *Karl Marx's Theory of History: a defence* (Oxford 1978); also, in this general area, S. Lukes, *Marxism and Morality* (Oxford 1985).

[1] This, of course, is a familiar theme. The working class under twentieth-century western capitalism has, generally, done too well to engender revolutionary activity. See also Claus Offe, *Disorganised Capitalism* (Oxford 1986) on this theme.

[2] For example, Alan Ryan in *Property and Political Theory* (Oxford 1984), 189-90.

[3] See J. Scott, *Capitalist Property and Financial Power* (Brighton 1986).

but a different form of owner-controlled enterprise. He
identifies the idea of 'impersonal ownership' to capture the
point that the owners of the largest modern businesses are
often other enterprises in turn owned by yet others. This chain
of ownership may be circular, as it weaves its way through the
business community, but that does not matter, for it signifies a
form of ownership that is connected with relations of power in
as direct a way as the classical nineteenth-century family firm.
I shall return to Scott's analysis below. It points to a lack of
accountability in business ownership that is becoming more
common and perhaps dangerous as the activities of ownership
come to resemble more a complicated financial game than a
concern with the particular company in hand. Scott's picture of
the role ownership plays in the financial strategies (not
manufacturing strategies) of large corporations is, of course,
familiar to most people from the occasional scandals and
charges of, asset-stripping, take-overs etc., that reach the
national newspapers.[1] This aspect of Scott's research connects
with the recent analysis of the international financial markets
provided by Susan Strange.[2]

(iv) Depending on whose analysis one accepts, and depending
on the size of firm in question (Scott's researches were based on
the largest companies in the three economies of Japan, USA
and the UK) it might be questioned whether ownership is as
directly connected with control as classically assumed.
Nevertheless, even if ownership and control are separate,
under a system of collective ownership someone will have to
assume the role of decision-maker and learn and apply
traditional entrepreneurial skills. As noted under (ii) above, if
we allow such skills as part of the labouring process, as they
surely are, it may just turn out that they require a
proportionately larger return on the value created in order to
ensure their continuing supply compared with the skills of the
shopfloor worker. So once again, the question of the ownership

---

[1] A recent example of the latter activity is the takeover of the family-run
chocolate manufacturers Rowntrees of York by the Swiss-based multinational,
Nestlé.

[2] S. Strange, *Casino Capitalism* (Oxford 1986). For specific details of how
computers are learning to join in the games, dealing in stocks and
commodities, see the *Guardian*, 5 August 1986.

of capital is separable from issues about the fairness of the distribution of rewards accruing to the various categories of worker that contribute to create the value *V*.

(v) Finally, without some connection between ownership and control in the economy, it is not at all clear that any form of planning adequate to running the economy efficiently is viable. There are three aspects to this familiar worry: (a) The incentive question; (b) problems of scale; and (c) the problem of accountability. (a) and (b) are matters that look to criticise any alternative to private ownership.

(a) is familiar from popular criticisms of East European states and, despite its naïve assumption that the only motivation for work is profit, there is no doubt that the monolithic state enterprises in East European countries and also in the nationalised industries of the UK have encountered severe problems of internal efficiency. However, it is a moot point whether this has more to do with the bureaucratisation due to the enormous size of the industry, or with a direct link with the lack of profit motivation.[1]

(b) is the problem encountered by governments of all political persuasions in the modern world; national economies (not to mention international economic affairs) are becoming simply too vast and complex to be brought under adequate control, be it the control of a central party bureaucracy or the legislature of a democratically elected government.

(c) The issue of accountability is slightly different. In the sort of scenario of ownership relations described by Scott and the ensuing gamelike strategies of the financial markets described by Strange, although ownership may connect with control the economy is not efficiently run or planned with regard to manufacturing production, because of the lack of accountability on the owners for the consequences of their pursuit of advantage in the money markets and take-over deals. Where we have a system of impersonal ownership the only constraint on economic planning is that of maximising profit regardless of the consequences for the manufacturing base of the economy. Of course, this is a problem within a traditional capitalist

---

[1] For a careful analysis of some of the issues involved here, see J. Vickers & G. Yarrow, *Privatization: an economic analysis* (Cambridge, Mass. 1988).

system, but there the capitalist has a concern not only to maximise her profits, but also to safeguard her enterprise and its continued contribution to the overall wealth of the nation. She may not have a direct concern for her workforce, but she is at least concerned that she remain in the position of having a workforce. Not so with the impersonal ownership relations so characteristic of contemporary capitalism. If enterprise *A* owns enterprise *B* but can enjoy greater profits by selling *B* in favour of *C* then it will do so regardless of whether *C* is a manufacturing enterprise directly concerned with the production of wealth or, instead, a service enterprise like insurance. In the schemes of impersonal ownership that are found today, the business of profit maximisation proceeds at such an abstract and rarefied level that is so removed from the manufacturing base that the owner no longer has even the traditional capitalist's interest in having a workforce; that is, a wealth-creating workforce rather than a service workforce. Of course, even this impersonal owner has an interest in there being a wealth-creating workforce; but if more profit can be made without one, far better that it be someone else's workforce that engages in the primary wealth-creation. As long as someone has a workforce large enough to warrant the services on offer, the impersonal owner is content to proceed with the abstract game of profit maximisation. In the terms of social choice theorists, the impersonal owner will free-ride on the various historical and cultural attachments that keep other owners tied to the manufacturing base. Without the historical and cultural attachments that keep owners tied to various manufacturing enterprises, this free-rider problem would become a many-person prisoner dilemma game. Collectively, it would be in everyone's interest if owners all took a share in primary wealth creation, even if greater profits were possible in service enterprises given a sufficiently large primary sector. However, without historical attachments etc., each owner could reason that *she* would do best by free-riding on the others' serving the collective interest. And if one can reason thus, all can. In consequence we would get a migration from the manufacturing base even more pronounced than the one that has taken place in the UK.[1] In the UK this has given

---

[1] According to W. Eltis & R. Bacon, *Britain's Economic Problem* (Basingstoke

the peculiar picture of a declining manufacturing base, rising unemployment *and* rising prosperity and success in the rarefied service industries of finance and insurance. This is Susan Strange's world of casino capitalism, where the pursuit of profit continues unattached and unaccountable to the demands of primary wealth-creation. The nub is that despite the gamelike atmosphere of this casino, decisions about currency exchange rates, interest rates, etc., have a direct influence on the manufacturing base, when high interest rates put whole enterprises out of business.

These then are some of the problems that beset the attempt to provide an analysis of the role of private ownership of capital in political theory and the requirement on socialism to combat this ownership. I shall not combat these problems directly, for I do not think that ownership is the real problem. When my analysis of the problem with capitalism is in place these problems will be left as obstacles to those who persist in thinking that ownership and equity of distribution are the key issues in criticising capitalism. In order to clear the decks for the critique of capitalism I shall offer we need still to dispose of the charge of alienation and exploitation. Like others I shall offer such charges, but they are usually tied up with the question of the ownership of capital. Before I can develop my account of alienation and exploitation these concepts must be untied from the flotsam and jetsam of obsolete worries. That is the next task on our agenda.

4. Alienation and exploitation

A common way of putting the supposed problem with the private ownership of capital is in terms of the twin concepts of alienation and exploitation. I shall begin with a brief outline of a common way of employing these concepts. I shall then, in §5, outline some problems with this and, in §6, criticise the liberal account of exploitation and alienation. Having done that I shall turn to a socialist account in §7. At that point the analytic socialist critique of capitalism, suggested in the last chapter, will be defended.

1976), the relative decline of the manufacturing base, that is as a percentage of GNP, is well entrenched.

In the industrial process all value is created by the activity of labouring (the labour theory of value). However, the labourer receives only a fraction of the value created, sufficient only to propagate her class and ensure a continuing supply of labour. The rest of the value created is taken by the capitalist not in virtue of any labour she has done, but only in virtue of her ownership of capital. This surplus value accrues to the capitalist solely in virtue of her ownership of capital. As such, the worker is exploited as the capitalist receives the bulk of the value produced without engaging in the labouring process. The worker receives a far smaller proportion. The worker is exploited, not because she does not receive a fair share, but because the bulk of what has been created by her labour is taken from her by the capitalist. Other than that proportion of the total value created which has already been acknowledged as required for reinvestment (including payment for entrepreneurial skills) and reward to the labourer, the value goes to someone who had no role in the creation of value. Unless there is some good reason why ownership of capital should grant ownership rights upon this surplus value, the worker whose work determines the size of the surplus looks to have as good a claim as anyone. In which case, the worker does not receive what is hers.

Because of this exploitation the worker is alienated. For the object produced by her labour, that into which she put herself, is taken from her and becomes opposed to her in the form of the wealth and power of the capitalist. Indeed the worker creates herself as an object of value, a commodity, and thereby also creates herself as something alien, to be owned and exchanged by the capitalist.

That suffices, I think, to give the barest outline of the concepts of exploitation and alienation. I do not think that such a description is as true of the industrial process today as it was in the nineteenth century. That such a description is not so accurate today is due to a host of problems readily identifiable in the above. I shall identify them in the next section before developing the liberal concepts of exploitation and alienation. Let me now colour the above description with a some quotations from Marx's *Economic and Philosophic Manuscripts of 1844*:

In the section on alienated labour he wrote:[1]

> The worker becomes poorer the more wealth he produces ... The *devaluation* of the human world increases in direct relation with the *increase in value* of the world of things. Labour does not only create goods; it also produces itself and the worker as a *commodity*, and indeed in the same proportion as it produces goods.

And:[2]

> This fact simply implies that the object produced by labour, its product, now stands opposed to it as an *alien being*, as a *power independent* of the producer.

Finally:[3]

> The more the worker expends himself in work the more powerful becomes the world of objects which he creates in face of himself, the poorer he becomes in his inner life, and the less he belongs to himself. It is just the same as in religion. The more of himself man attributes to God the less he has left in himself.

5. Alienation and exploitation: some problems

From the all too brief description of the industrial process in §4 it may well seem that the immediate and obvious answer to the problem of alienation and exploitation is the removal of the capitalist class. That is, if we remove those who exploit and alienate workers simply by virtue of their ownership of capital, will it not be the case that the alienation and exploitation will cease?[4] After all, if the total value created by the labouring process could be returned to the worker (save that required for re-investment), she would not be exploited and would not be alienated either, for her surplus value would not be treated as a commodity to be accumulated and exchanged by the

---

[1] K. Marx, *Economic and Philosophic Manuscripts 1844* (London 1973), 121.
[2] Op. cit., 122.
[3] Ibid.
[4] That is, we remove the power-hold the capitalist has over the working class – 'Capital is ... the power of command over labour and its products. The capitalist possesses this power, not on account of his personal or human qualities, but as the *owner* of capital', op. cit., 85.

capitalist class. This naïve and crude solution attempts a tight connection between the question of the private ownership of capital and the theory of socialism: the workers will be liberated from alienation and exploitation by the abolition of the private ownership of capital. Presumably this will pass into some form of social ownership, though let us leave that problem untouched for the moment. However, it is not, of course, as simple as that, and the complexities I have in mind are not practical ones to do with the application of theory to the real world, they are theoretical complexities to do with the adequacy of the theory.

Let us first note that in the crude description of the industrial process in §4 and the very general remedy noted above, the concepts of alienation and exploitation, whatever roughness there may be to their contours, have some definite characteristics. In the first place, the workers suffer exploitation not because they do not receive a fair share of their product, but because they do not receive what is theirs. This is worth noting:

(5) Exploitation occurs when the workers do not receive what is rightly theirs.

(5) is important for marking the scientific not utopian character of Marx's concept of exploitation. It is not the abstract moral concept of fairness which underpins the concept of exploitation, it is the removal of that which already belongs to the worker. Secondly, the concept of alienation also has a scientific element which we do well to separate from the more familiar everyday use of the idea. Alienation is not simply the idea of the worker failing to find meaning in her work and thereby feeling alienated in it; *that* is what I call the liberal concept of alienation. I shall turn to it shortly. Alienation is more precisely to do with the way in which the worker in capitalism finds the product of her labour, the object of value which she created and is hers (indeed into which she has put herself) *turned against her* as the capitalist appropriates this object and turns it into capital. This is the point of the quotation above from p. 122 of the 1844 manuscripts. Again, it is worth noting:

(6) Alienation occurs when the worker's labour is turned against her.

Now, as remarked, there are several theoretical problems with the crude sketch given in §4. Meeting these problems rapidly takes us into the liberal use of the concepts of alienation and exploitation which both loses the preciseness of (5) and (6) and also the connection between alienation/exploitation and ownership.

One of the first things to be noted with the description in §4 is that although it may have been true in the nineteenth century that the worker received only a subsistence wage, 'sufficient only to propagate her class and ensure a continuing supply of labour', it is not true today. In the industrialised western economies collective bargaining has brought about a far greater share of the created value for the worker than is allowed in §4. So, the first problem with §4 is this:

> (a) Does the worker only get subsistence wages? If she does not, why can not collective bargaining produce all of the share of the product of her labour that is hers?

The second question raised in (a) is not a practical but a theoretical one. That is, if collective bargaining can so increase the workers' share of the product of their labour to contemporary western proportions, why should it be necessary to abolish private ownership of capital to ensure that the worker gets her full share? This is an important point, for unless one thought that the capitalist was due no share of the created value at all (I shall come to that point next) why could it not be the case that the workers could obtain their full share by that same process which has to date increased their share many times over? Again, I want to stress the theoretical intent of this problem, not its practical application, for its theoretical interest is no more than the problem of whether or not exploitation can be remedied without the abolition of the private ownership of capital.

Quite how one decides this first problem will depend, in part, on the second issue I want to raise from the description in §4. Is it true to say that the capitalist does not take part in the labouring process? In raising this question it is important that it is not confused with a quite separate question already dealt with: namely, does the *entrepreneur* take part in the labouring process? I have already answered that in the affirmative, and that is just to acknowledge that 'workers' covers both 'workers by hand and by brain'.[1] The present issue is whether the capitalist, in virtue of owning capital can be said to take a part in the process that creates value. This issue is perhaps better approached from the other side by asking instead the following question which also naturally arises from the description of §4:

(b) Why is the wealth created by the worker hers?

This can seem like a naïve question, but it is not. Although labour might be the only source of those things – commodities – that have value, it does not follow that it is the sole creator of that value, or that it is the sole owner of value. What argument is there to suggest that capitalists are due some return of the value created; that is, that there is a legitimate proportion of the total value created that should go to the owner of capital? One argument would be this. The creation of value by the worker could not take place without capital, it is labour *plus* capital that produces value. However, this thought can be rebutted by observing that it is capital that is required, not capitalists. But that is not conclusive, for if capital is required some agency must supply it, even if that agency is the central party apparatus which owns the capital on behalf of all. Whatever agency supplies the capital, ensures that it is kept in good order, organises the investment programme, plans production levels and so on, that agency will require and be entitled to some return on its labour. That is to say, the agency will be a party to the labouring process, and as such the wealth created by the worker is not all hers, for it belongs, in part, to those who share in the labouring process, whether party officials or capitalists.

This still misses the point. The argument only grants a return to the entrepreneurial skills of capitalists or party officials, it does not yet grant a return in virtue of *ownership*. We have to be clear to keep these points distinct. Here is a further argument that suggests that ownership of capital, not entrepreneurial skills, licenses an income from the total value created. Take the case of the ownership of industrial capital. In such a case capital is the machinery and buildings employed in

---

[1] As the infamous Clause 4 of the British Labour Party constitution insists.

the manufacturing process. Let us concentrate on machinery. Consider the machinery m employed in industrial process P. This machinery is the product of some earlier process P_{-1}. Suppose now that the workers in this earlier process jointly own m because their creation of m gives them ownership rights in m. Now if they own m, it is theirs to do with as they see fit; for example, they could exchange it for money. This value of m we can designate as V. Now, if in creating and coming to own m these workers are licensed to obtain V in return for parting with m, why could they not part with it in the following way. Rather than sell m and obtain V all in one go, they set up the industrial process P with a different group of workers who, in working on m, create an extra value V^*. The original group now recoup the value V due them for having created m in the first place as a return upon their investment of m in the process P and as a proportion of the new value V^*. Let me call the ownership the original workers have of m, *primary ownership*. That is, it is ownership that arises from receiving the full fruits of one's labour. Where the capital invested in an industrial process is placed there by someone who has a primary ownership of the capital, it seems they have a right, due to this ownership, to expect a proportion of whatever value is created by the employment of the capital by further workers. This is a right to a return from that value that accrues, not because of entrepreneurial skills, but because of ownership. Furthermore it is a right that is grounded in the labour theory of value, for it is that which grants the reward due to the workers who produced m in the first place.

If such primary ownership is legitimately due a reward from the value created in the industrial process, so too will all sorts of secondary, tertiary, etc., ownerships under appropriate conditions. For example, suppose the workers in process P_{-1} sell their holding in m to some group G. G now have a legitimate holding in m and are thereby entitled to the value residing in m. Once more, if they are entitled to that value by sale of m, why not also by rent, when the rent is achieved by way of a return on investment? Such entitlement to a return from investment licensed by *ownership* of the invested capital seems justified. Furthermore it is justified in a manner that appeals to the principles of the labour theory of value which underpins the concept of primary ownerhsip in terms of which all other ownership claims are derived inductively.

There is an exception to this argument, and it is this: What about the ownership of land? The notion of primary ownership employed above granted ownership rights in the machinery *m* through the labours of the original workforce that created *m*. It is that original creation which is appealed to in validating the further ownership rights and dues that arise as *m* is exchanged between agents. But in the case of land, its value is not so plausibly seen as deriving from a creative act of labour. Ownership claims to land often derive from no more than the historical accident that one person, rather than another, got there first. If that is the case, the appeal to the labour theory of value will not justify income due to ownership. The problem here is this.

The above argument justified income derived from ownership because, in effect, it suggested a way of treating unearned income as derivable from earned income. An agent's right to an income derived from labour and earned by the principles of the labour theory of value is deferred by exchange and so becomes a right to an unearned income from the capital that can be traced to the original labour which justifies the eventual claim. With land, all too often, there is no original labour to anchor the claim: more likely just a bloody feud. Land, then, seems to be a special case, and I think that is right. The point could be contested if we distinguished between those holdings in land which originate with a genuine working on the land to create the original value and right to receive that value, and those holdings which originate in some accidental feature, such as who reached the land first. However, I shall not pursue the analysis of holdings in land here. For one thing, in our industrial society, although land ownership is important and spectacularly large holdings often cause great offence to many, land itself is not so important for the analysis of capitalism I want to develop. What *is* important about land is the way that, with the emergence of capitalism, it became treated as a *commodity*, rather than something with a fixed value and place within society. With the emergence of capitalism land was freed from the bonds of feudalism under which, no matter how inequitable the distribution, it had a contributory though not necessarily beneficial role to play in delimiting the contours of social life. I shall return to this point in §8.

In conclusion, the labour theory of value does not sustain a use of the concepts of alienation and exploitation that makes a sharp connection between the patterns of capital ownership in society and a socialist critique of those patterns. I turn now to examine briefly the liberal account of these critiques, before outlining what *is* wrong with capitalism.

6. Alienation and exploitation: the liberal account

We have seen that the idea that the private ownership of capital inherently fosters exploitation and alienation is not without problems. Of course, one might put the whole point against capitalism in terms of moral ideals of fairness and equality, but that is not the way I wish to proceed for I do not think it viable.[1] Nevertheless I wish to argue that we can employ the concepts of alienation and exploitation in a way that requires the abolition of capitalism *as a means of social organisation not ownership*. But first, we must be clear to distinguish the case from that of the liberal.

The liberal employs the concepts of alienation and exploitation but without the features noted in §5 as characteristic of their use by Marx, features (5) and (6). In contrast to such a use the liberal is marked by speaking of alienation and exploitation in a way that grounds their use in a appeal to moral ideals, specifically fairness when discussing exploitation and a lack of a meaningful life when using alienation. I have already remarked that, whether or not it is useful to speak of exploitation when the worker does not receive a fair share of the product of her labour, it is not Marx's use. It is however a popular use.

More striking and perhaps familiar is the liberal notion of alienation. This is typified in a recent book by Ryan on the role of property in political theory.[2] In the final chapter Ryan asks, 'Why are there so few socialists?' With regard to the concept of alienation his answer relies on the claim that modern industrial life is so vastly improved on that of the nineteenth century which Marx witnessed that much of the horror of

---

[1] I consider these concepts and the role they play in socialism at greater length in Chapter 5.

[2] Ryan, *Property and Political Theory*, op. cit.

industrial work has been alleviated. He notes:[1]

> This is not to say that a shorter working day has created the
> unalienated man of Marx's vision – we do not find our working
> lives such a central part of our lives as Marx had hoped – but
> that the horrors of what Marx called an alienated life have been
> vastly reduced.

This claim is confusing in a number of respects. First, it is not
clear what Ryan has in mind by 'alienation'. In the aside in the
centre of the quoted passage he may be thinking of the true
Marxist concept of alienation which embodies (6) above. For if
we do not find our work a central part of our lives there is
perhaps some ground for thinking that the worker's labouring
conditions still allow for the product of her labour to be turned
against her. But this is not clear. And anyhow, it is far from
fruitful to think of the unalienated life as one where the worker
can enjoy complete absorption in her labour. Such an idea too
easily slips into the utopian mode of thought and fosters the
notion that true unalienated labour is to be found only in the
small workshops of skilled artisans. This is dangerous
nonsense. The concept of alienation, if it is to serve any useful
purpose in an analysis of modern industrial society, must allow
scope for unalienated industrial labour even when some such
labour is essentially boring. There is more to the concept of
alienation than finding one's work intrinsically boring. This is
not to say that this psychological aspect of the concept of
alienation is to be ignored, only that it should not be taken as
definitive.

In the second place, the quoted passage is unclear in so far
as, although there is some recognition of a notion of alienation
that embodies (6), the respects in which Ryan thinks modern
workers have seen the horrors of alienation reduced are all to
do with the psychologistic aspect of the concept. Ryan
catalogues the improvements in working conditions since
Marx's time – shorter working day, better housing, better
safety care in factories, etc. – and concludes that 'the amount of
sheer toil has been steadily diminishing'.[2] But this is just to
emphasise the psychologistic aspect of alienation and make it

[1] Ibid., 184.
[2] Ibid.

seem as if the horror of capitalism is simply that of getting one's hands dirty doing other people's dirty work for the other people's profit. Of course, one can feel terribly upset at such an arrangement, but that alone hardly constitutes an argument against capitalism. Any argumentative force in observing that that is the way things are in industry would have to derive from sources other than such a concept of alienation. It may be that under capitalism a majority are forced to get grubby hands for the pleasure and profit of the minority, but unless we have an antecedent conception of how this is unfair and an inequitable distribution of the burdens of labour, we have nothing of an argument here.

It is just such a moral base in the concept of fairness that typifies the liberal employment of the concept of alienation that ties it up with the liberal idea of exploitation mentioned above. The liberal will think that there is a criticism implicit in observing that the majority are dirtying their hands for the pleasure of the minority just because she will think that this is unfair. Well, it may be unfair; but if it is, we need an argument to say why. The liberal will, familiarly, be met with the counter-observation that in thereby doing the minority's dirty work the workers are well remunerated. Collective bargaining has paid off handsomely and, furthermore, the majority are happy with their lot. Of course, this is all contentious and the battleground for many a contemporary debate. It is, moreover, a morass of tangled assumptions and differing concepts of alienation and exploitation, and it is not my aim to untie this particular Gordian knot. I think a more profitable critique of capitalism can be defended without relying on the abstract moral sentiments of the liberal.[1]

The liberal concept of alienation is then characterised something like this:

(7) alienation occurs when the worker is required to perform boring, meaningless work.

As an observation this may be true, as a definition it is hopeless. It encourages the idea that what matters in

---

[1] In Chapter 6 I shall turn to consider one important and famous liberal argument to the effect that present arrangements are unfair: namely, that due to John Rawls in his *A Theory of Justice* (Oxford 1970).

contemporary industrial society is not the pattern of ownership, but the pattern of control and bureaucracy. As Ryan points out, it was the bureaucratisation of management and organisations, not ownership, that Weber seized on as typical of capitalism in contrast to Marx. It is Ryan's Weberian conclusion that 'what makes work drudgery owes more to technique than ownership'[1] that I wish to resist as a central plank of socialism. Indeed I do not even want to make a fuss about drudgery as such.

There are two aspects to the liberal concept of alienation, both of which surface in Ryan's book. One is the idea that alienation occurs through lack of control in the work process. However, it is far from clear that there is a simple connection between finding work meaningful and having control over the work and the working conditions.[2] But however the technical issues here are resolved, there is a good deal of plausibility in Ryan's observation that 'so long as the cow has been producing plenty of milk nobody has been very excited about who decided when to milk her'.[3] The second aspect is simply that of the meaninglessness of much industrial work where this is not further characterised as lack of control, but simply a lack of *point*, from the worker's point of view. Again, there is a quantity of research done on this issue and whether or not, for example, redesign of production lines can repair the lack of point.[4] But on a wider canvass, again there is something to Ryan's observation:[5]

> The ordinary person does not lead a meaningless or an amoral or an apathetic life; but the meaning of his life, what engages his moral energies and his attention, are largely domestic concerns.

This observation introduces us to an important fact about contemporary social life, one that will now point us in the right direction for a critique of capitalism.

Earlier, in the same chapter, Ryan observes:[6]

---

[1] Op. cit., 19.
[2] For a discussion of some of the issues involved here, see J. Child, *Organization* (New York 1984), esp. chs. 8, 9.
[3] Op. cit., 185.
[4] For a sympathetic account of the gains to be had from job redesign, see J. Hackman & G. Oldham, *Work Redesign* (Reading, Mass. 1980).
[5] Op. cit., 187.
[6] Op. cit., 179.

Three men digging in the same hole to locate gas, water and
electricity mains, will be acutely aware of differentials in their
pay; about the wealth of Lord Cowdray they neither know nor
care.

Ryan explains this point availing himself of the notion of a
'reference group' as employed by Runciman that I introduced
in Chapter 1 in my account of the grounding of the good life.[1]
Runciman's point was that when an individual or group has a
grievance to voice, this grievance is expressed relative to a
particular reference group. What is more, such reference
groups for grievances are normally socially and economically
close. Workers in one car plant express their grievances over
pay and conditions employing similar workers in another car
plant as their reference group, not by reference to the pay of
high court judges. This point about the closeness of reference
groups for grievances, as also the closeness of the concerns that
make for a meaningful life, is important.

7. Alienation from the good and the aristocracy of capital

We have come a long way now in pursuing the claims that
socialism should be founded upon a critique of the private
ownership of capital. These claims are not successful. In place
of them I can now offer an analytic critique of capitalism that
has no need of the liberal's moral base for the charges of
alienation and exploitation.

The central indictment of capitalism is this: Under
capitalism, the labouring subject must be freed from the
normative bonds that would otherwise hold her in place within
the community. If this is not done, the 'labour market' cannot
be established as a commodity market. If it *is* done, the
possibility that human life will be structured by moral norms is
shattered. And upon this indictment we may frame the
following account of alienation:

Under capitalism the subject is alienated from the norms
that alone can provide a human social life framed by
moral values, the subject is alienated from the good.

[1] Cf. W.G. Runciman, *Relative Deprivation and Social Justice* (London
1972), ch. 2.

More briskly:

*Under capitalism life is lived not under the Authority of
the Good, but under the aristocracy of capital.*

This charge is not offered as an empirical observation. Rather
it is derived from *a priori* reflection upon the nature of moral
life and the nature of society once it accepts a capitalistic
arrangement of the economy. It is important to be clear on this
point, for it is no refutation of the argument to point to
someone, or some group, that is succeeding with a good life
under capitalism. My claim is not that it is impossible for an
individual to be good under capitalism. That would be silly. My
claim is that it is not possible for society to be good under
capitalism. Here and there individuals may flourish and
spread some of their virtue among others. But even those who
do flourish and find the resources to flourish *for* others are
ultimately demeaned by the fact that their flourishing must go
on within a vacuum. They do not flourish within a civil order of
the good. And in such barren conditions it is not surprising
that it is often difficult to flourish with civility and humility.
Far easier to block out the street-corner punks and the decrepit
slum dwellers, the state-sanctioned destitute living on mean
benefit provision and the mass of economically and emotionally
battered victims of the cruel inner city shrines to Capital's
pleasure. The indictment is a charge against the moral health
of *society as a whole*, and it is made on *a priori* grounds. Let me
clarify those grounds.

First, what constitutes a capitalistic arrangement of an
economy? Now by 'capitalism' I mean a society organised for
the needs of Capital. The needs of Capital are those
arrangements which allow the greatest potential for profit-
making; *that* is the logic of Capital. In order for Capital to be
able to pursue the maximum profits wherever and whenever
they occur, it must be free from various sorts of restrictions.
The sort of restrictions we need to consider here may be
classified according to the agents involved.

An economy is an arrangement between agents of various
sorts. A capitalist economy is one in which the only
requirement is that the agents be arranged in such a way to
allow for the maximum realisation of profit. For this to be the

case, various ties between agents that would otherwise constrain their economic activity must be broken. The most dramatic and important case is that of the human agents who make up the labour force of an economy. In contrast, a society, a civil society, is an arrangement of agents where the agents are bound by ties other than that of competitors in the labour market. That is, a civil society requires moral agency and not just economic agency.

If Capital is to be able to pursue maximum profits, the labour power of human beings must be treated as a commodity, something to be exchanged, bought and sold solely on the criterion of whether or not a particular exchange increases the profit ratio of the enterprise concerned. Now, as has been pointed out, the labour power of a human agent is unlike other commodities.[1] Labour power suffers from an inelasticity of supply unlike, for example, manufactured commodities or raw material. Labour power is but a quality of a living human being and, as such, is not something that can be simply 'turned off' if demand slumps. Nor, for that matter, can it be 'turned on' readily when demand peaks.

Labour power is an abstract property of human beings. It is their potential for producing value when placed in a work situation. For it to remain a property of human beings it must be considered secondary to those properties that constitute human life. If the labour power of humans is given precedence to those properties that constitute human social life, it is no longer a property of *humans*, for it has then become constitutive, a defining property, of its supplier. The labour power of a human being is *not* its defining or constitutive property: treating it as such dehumanises us literally. In treating it as such the economic arrangement of agents replaces and overshadows the arrangement of agents in a civil society. But when we live in an economy organised under the aristocracy of Capital, our labour power *must* become our defining property on pain of failure of that economy.

[1] See Karl Polanyi, *Origins of Our Times: the great transformation* (London 1945), esp. ch. 6 for the analysis that labour power is a *fictitious* commodity. Polanyi's analysis has been picked up enthusiastically by Claus Offe, particularly in his *Disorganised Capitalism* (Cambridge & Oxford 1985); see especially chs. 1, 2. Polanyi did not restrict his charge of 'fictitious commodity' to labour, but included also land and money as commodity fictions. In this I think he was right and I give reasons for this below.

My only assumption in this argument is this. Human beings are creatures who essentially live a life with a purpose, a point and meaning supplied by their moral codes. However such codes may vary, and however they may bring us in conflict with one another; what makes us human is the attempt to live according to the moral norms that shape our lives and social institutions. We find a moral point to the world and our progress through it. That is what makes us human. In short, we live, or attempt to live, according to the authority of the good. We live, or attempt to live, in a civil society. But when we live in a society which is moulded to suit the economic interests of Capital, this is not possible. For then our labour power becomes treated as our defining property instead of our moral power – our ability to live according to the authority of the good. And it is then that we forfeit the authority of the good for the aristocracy of Capital. For the logic of Capital, the profit motive, to be applied properly according to its own dictates, our moral powers and the authority of the good must be denied.

It is this dethronement of the moral life by the aristocracy of Capital that constitutes the main charge against capitalism construed now not as a claim about ownership patterns, but structurally, as in definition (1), as a claim about the organisation of society. The general point to this critique is this. Human agents possess various goals that arise from their nature as social beings with a moral life, a life bounded by moral norms that acknowledge the authority of the good. These goals provide us with the reference groups that make up our social life; they provide the ties that hold social life together. Under a capitalist economy these arrangement have to be supplanted by the profit motive and the competitive vacuum which arranges people only by virtue of their labour power divorced from the reference groups that define human life. For, to capitalism, these reference groups are a restriction; to us, they are the stuff of moral life. If the reference groups are not supplanted, Capital cannot pursue its goal of profit maximisation. It is this dethronement of the authority of the Good, the reference groups, that stands at the base of the socialist critique of capitalism. Stripped of the reference groups which carry our social and moral life, naked before the advancing juggernaut of capitalism and flailed by the profit motive, we stand bare of the protection afforded by the norms of moral life;

we stand bared of a moral life at all. And we cannot reclothe with moral norms until Capital is restrained. For, by the argument of Chapter 1, the only source of moral norms lies in our traditions and communities; it is not in the individual. So there is no return to the moral life by the bare economic agent choosing various norms. The norms must come first, and for that Capital must be restricted in its operations.

The general point concerning the replacement of reference groups peculiar to the viability of the agents concerned by the aristocracy of capital applies to other sorts of agents in society beside human beings. For example, consider the agencies of the media. If, for example, television is to meet its generally accepted role as objective purveyor of news and supplier of entertainment there are certain criteria that are to be employed in measuring the success of any particular TV company. These criteria supply us with the reference groups appropriate for assessment of programme supply. Doubtless the criteria required are matters of considerable debate. For example, what constitutes 'quality' entertainment and good drama? Nevertheless, however argument may rage over the exact nature of these criteria, we believe they exist and we argue about them. And it is important that we do. As long as we continue to argue about the appropriate criteria by which to judge our public broadcasting services those services have a healthy future; for then, at least, the prospect that such services might bow to the authority of the criteria for good public broadcasting remains alive. However, once our broadcasting industry is turned over wholly to the criteria of the market and the profit motive and *that* is made the dominant criterion for success, the future of broadcasting is irreparably dimmed. From the perspective of the profit motive, the reference groups over which we argue in assessing the value of our programme supply are a restriction. Such reference groups promote goals other than, and at variance with, the maximisation of profit. These reference groups must survive if public broadcasting is to have any chance of meeting its purpose. And note, the criticism here is not that a market approach to broadcasting violates some specific standard, it is that such an approach denies the applicability of there being any reference groups, any non-profit-oriented goals for broadcasting at all, regardless of which particular goals you happen to favour. The criticism begs no assumptions about the particular goals of broadcasting, as earlier I begged no assumption about the goals of human social life. In each case I assume only that there are such things as the goals necessary to good public broadcasting and the goals necessary to human life lived under the authority of the Good, and that such goals are encoded in our reference groups and the traditions they supply.

From these two examples we can generalise the critique of capitalism in the following way. Within society there are agents of various kinds. Agency brings with it assumptions about the goals and standards of action constitutive of being an agent of such-and-such a kind. Such goals are delimited by the reference groups peculiar to each kind of agency. The standards of action are found in traditions encoded within these reference groups. Without those goals and their attendant reference groups and traditions one cannot be an agent of the appropriate kind. However, under capitalism, where the economy is primarily arranged for the benefit of Capital, these various reference groups which define the different agencies we meet in human social life constitute restrictions to the logic of Capital. From the point of view of what is constitutive of such agencies, the profit motive is a disruptive intrusion into the fabric of goals and standards provided by the reference groups peculiar to a given form of agency. The economy supplants society.

The goal for Capital, the only goal, is the maximisation of profit, and that can only be adequately pursued if the reference groups that bind agents of different kinds together are disbanded. Labour power must be 'freed' from the moral life. But for the moral life to survive, for the reference groups and traditions to flourish, Capital must be restricted. We need to renew the criteria and goals that preserve the moral life over and above the economisation of that life by capitalism. We need to rekindle the authority of the good and dethrone the aristocracy of Capital.

8. The 1844 manuscripts

Hints of the above line of argument can be found in Marx's early writings. Marx acknowledged the romantic appeal of feudalism over capitalism. The arrival of the latter occurred with the 'transformation of the land into a commodity ... and the complete triumph of the aristocracy of money'.[1] The transition is one in which 'landed property, the *root* of private property, should be drawn completely into the movement of private property and become a *commodity* ... that the rule of the property owner should appear as the *naked rule of private property* of capital, dissociated from all political colouring'.[2] Note how Marx identifies landed property as the root of private property. They are not the same. The latter comes about only when land is treated as a commodity, disconnected from any political or moral colouring to the ownership relation. We might put this by saying that under feudalism the relation between landowner and serf is not wholly economised; there are reference groups which they share and which give a moral contour to their relationship. Indeed simply being a serf or a master defines one's role within the typical feudal reference group; being a serf carries certain codes of behaviour with it.

Marx elaborates that under capitalism the relation between property owner and worker is[3]

> confined to the economic relationship of exploiter and exploited; that all personal relationships between the property owner and his property should cease, and the latter become purely *material* wealth; that in place of the honourable marriage with the land there should be a marriage of interest, and the land as well as man himself be reduced to the level of an object of speculation.

This is in contrast to feudalism:[4]

> The rule of landed property does not ... appear as the direct rule of capital. Its dependents stand to it more in the relation in which stand to their fatherland.

In feudalism[5]

> there is the appearance of a more intimate connection between the owner and the land than is the case in the possession of mere *wealth*. Landed property assumes an individual character with its lord ... It appears as the inorganic body of its lord.

[1] *1844 Manuscripts*, 113.
[2] Ibid. (Marx's emphasis).
[3] Ibid.
[4] Ibid., 114.
[5] Ibid.

Finally:[1]

> In such a situation [feudalism], labour still appears to have a
> *social* meaning, still has a significance of *genuine* communal life,
> and has not progressed to *neutrality* in relation to its content, to
> full self-sufficient being, i.e. to abstraction from all other
> existence and thus to liberated capital.

And:

> *Landed property*, as distinct from capital, is private property,
> capital, which is still afflicted by local and political prejudices; it
> is capital which has not yet emerged from its involvement with
> the world.

From these passages we can glean the following train of
thought of a kind with that suggested in the previous section.
It is only with the development of land as a commodity that
private property assumes a problematic character. This is due
to the economisation of relationships between human agents
that follows the treatment of land as a commodity. The worker
no longer stands as the serf did to the master in a relationship
that, whatever its faults, was one defined by shared reference
groups. Under capitalism the worker stands as one commodity
among others to be exchanged as seems fit for the
maximisation of profit which is, after all, the ultimate goal of
the capitalist organisation of society. But it is only with the
unfettering of capital from the chains of the various
involvements defined by reference groups that the profit
motive can come to assume the dominance it does under
capitalism. It is the dismantling of the weave of reference
groups that constrains ownership of property under, say,
feudalism, that frees Capital to pursue its goal of profit
maximisation and accumulation. That would not have been
possible without the breakdown of the moral life defined by the
weave of the reference groups. The return to the moral life will
not be possible without the dismantling of capitalism.

We should note that in one of the passages quoted Marx
speaks of the relation between owner and worker as confined to
the economic relation of exploiter and exploited. But we do not

[1] Ibid., 140 and 144.

need to invoke the labour theory of value and the idea that the worker is the sole owner of the value of the product of her labour to make her role that of the exploited. The point is this. With the total economisation of the relationship between owner and worker there are, as it were, 'no holds barred' to the determination of the relevant standing of the owner and worker. The worker is not, as under feudalism, part of the organic whole of the lord's estate, someone who has a clearly defined role within the reference groups of the estate, a role which determines in part questions about welfare, reward for labour and so on. Under capitalism the worker's role is defined solely as a commodity, an element to be paid for in the pursuit of profit and therefore, like any commodity in a market designed for the maximisation of profit, to be bought as cheaply as possible. In that sense we may say that the worker is exploited, for though her labour may not vary, the capitalist is always under pressure to obtain that very same amount of labour, and if possible more, for a smaller price. In that way the worker is exploited as she is treated as a commodity with no fixed value, and no reference groups, regardless of the values created in her labour. Of course, this is not to deny that under feudalism workers could be and were exploited in the liberal sense of not receiving a fair share of the product of their labour. The difference is that under capitalism, no matter how nice the capitalist may be, with the breakdown of the reference groups which define interpersonal exchanges, the gloves are off and the only thing that ultimately matters is for the capitalist to secure as high a return as possible on investment. This concern to maximise profits may, of course, be tempered by moral concerns for those who produce the value, but this is wholly accidental. The capitalist who tempers the profit motive with a concern for the workers is vulnerable to those competitors in the market who lack such concern. Market forces will require such soft-hearted capitalists to bow to the profit motive or go under.

As noted in the Introduction, until the post-war boom ended in 1973, it seemed that, given the ease with which profits could be made, many capitalists could afford non-capitalistic concerns for their workers. But since the end of that boom, tighter profit margins have revealed the true interests of Capital as market forces have taken bite and forced capitalists to attend to their *raison d'être*.

Of course, all this is not to indulge in a eulogy of feudalism any more than Marx did. Feudalism has certain advantages over capitalism in so far as there were other aspects to social relations than the purely economic. But there is no going back, and if we accept Marx's theory of history feudalism was destined to evolve into capitalism. However, the main lesson to be learnt from this analysis is that it is not the privacy of property under capitalism that matters, it is that capitalism treats private property as a commodity. This in turn entails that society be organised for the maximisation of profit as the ultimate goal and *that* brings about the total economisation of all social relations, the fragmentation of reference groups referred to in the previous section. This picture is apparent in Marx where, in the second manuscript, he says:[1]

> Production does not only produce man as a *commodity*, the human commodity, man in the form of a *commodity*; in conformity with this situation it produces him as a *mentally* and physically dehumanised being ... Immorality, miscarriage, helotism of workers and capitalists ... Its product is the *self-conscious* and *self-activating commodity* ... The *human* commodity ... It is a great step forward by Ricardo, Mill *et al.*, as against Smith and Say, to declare the *existence* of human beings as *indifferent* or indeed harmful. The true end of production is not the number of workers a given capital maintains, but the amount of interest it earns, the total annual savings.

And although Marx's recipe for escaping the problem of the economisation of social relations was the abolition of private property, the *point* of doing this is as identified in the present analysis:[2]

> *Communism* is the *positive* abolition of *private property*, of *human self-alienation*, and thus the real *appropriation* of *human* nature through and for man. It is, therefore, the return of man himself as a *social*, i.e. really human, being.

---

[1] Ibid., 138.
[2] Ibid., 155.

9. Alienation and exploitation revisited:
what has to be done

I have now completed the analytic critique of capitalism defined as a method of structuring human society. Its fault lies in its dehumanisation of society. The alienation that matters in modern society is not the liberal notion of finding work boring and meaningless, it is the alienation from the authority of the Good, that is what matters. And the notion of exploitation that matters is not a notion of fair reward for a day's labour, it is the exploitation that arises from having a human life reduced to that of a commodity to be purchased ever cheaper when the market allows.

If this is the critique, what has to be done? The main task for socialists must be this. We must rearticulate the criteria, the goals, that define our agency in the social world and which provide the reference groups which alone can carry the traditions necessary for moral life to proceed. We must rearticulate the authority of the Good. In doing this we must articulate the more specific goals and standards for the variety of human institutions we find in modern society and stand these goals in opposition to the market criteria of capitalist success. I have already mentioned the example of public broadcasting. Other obvious examples are health care, education, control of the environment, public services such as power, postage and water supply. In the UK at the time of writing all these things are facing the challenge of being subordinated to market criteria of capitalist success. If socialists cannot articulate the criteria by which they should be assessed we will soon find there is no human society left and the aristocracy of capital will be complete. And once we accept the idea that there are such reference groups which define our various purposes and whose goods and goals need elevating before the demands of Capital in order that the goods of human civil society can flourish, we can also begin to see our way to rewrite the key assumptions of political economy. For, as I have remarked on a couple of occasions, it is not obvious that the economic interests of small businesses are the same as the deregulated interests of Capital. Indeed on certain key points, for example currency exchange rates and interest rates, it seems only too likely that the goals and needs of many businesses are poorly served by the deregulation of financial markets which, from the abstract point of view of the needs of Capital, can seem such a good thing. There is scope for a new political economy of the business community which seeks to thrash out the criteria for their success and formulate the boundaries of their reference group. When this is done it may well turn out that the interests of many businesses amount to further restrictions on the logic of Capital. If the Left can escape their familiar knee-jerk responses to those who own modest amounts of capital they may yet find powerful allies in restructuring a regulated economy.[1]

In tackling this project of defending our various reference groups and their traditions from the logic of Capital a central role must be accorded to the state. I shall not defend that thought here, but most of the theoretical machinery to justify state action has already been made available at this point. For the state is probably the only agency with the power and resources to constrain the operation of Capital to defend the reference groups which define our various non-economic criteria of agency.[2] For now we need to address the theoretical question of what has to be the case for the appropriate arguments about the Good in general, and particular criteria of good also, to take place. I have argued that socialism requires an objective notion of the good life, but is this available? And, if it is, how do we go about evaluating the different and often incompatible traditions of the good that are thrown up when we allow our reference groups to flourish? That last question is, perhaps, the most fundamental challenge in social theory today. In the next chapter I show how it can be met.

[1] I shall return to this question in Chapter 7.
[2] But see my 'Bringing the state back in', *Political Quarterly* (July 1989).

3

Criticising Traditions:
solving *the* problem in social theory

I have argued that socialism should be founded on a concern to enable the good life to be lived, with the assumption that there is such a thing as *the* good life. This requires that we should be able to make sense of the idea that there are such things as objective moral values. Many people think that that idea is silly. In this chapter I show why it is not.

1. A tale of two problems

There are two problems that are commonly encountered in pressing the idea of the objectivity of our moral values. I shall call them the *relativity* problem and the *pluralism* problem. The first is a peculiarly philosophical problem that arises from a distorted metaphysical image, and although it has grossly infected the common consciousness, it is not, I believe, so difficult to eradicate. The pluralism problem has broader roots within our intuitive moral experience and will take more time to exorcise.

The relativity problem is this. When we say of some action that it is good, we are not describing something about the way the world is. Rather, we are expressing a reaction we have to the world. Values, so the thought goes, are not really part of the world, they are to do with the way we humans react to a world that is, considered in itself, morally inert. If we set out to produce a catalogue of all the things there are in the world, we would include the trees and stars, the stones and buildings, the plants and animals, but we would not include the moral values. For when we say that some action or agent is good we are

87

reporting the way we *feel* in response to a happening in the world that can be described, without loss, without mentioning the evaluative component which we 'add' to the morally inert world. Values then are subjective, for they are defined relatively to our particular sensitivities to the world; they are not part of the objective world.

The pluralism problem poses a challenge to objectivism about values that starts far nearer home. It goes like this. Even if we thought there was reason to doubt the kind of subjectivity of values raised by the relativity problem, we have to address the fact that we face the world embedded in radically different and often incompatible traditions. There seems to be an incommensurable plurality in our conceptions of what is morally valuable and what is not. Nomadic tribespeople are often found to endorse a value system that permits euthanasia while most western industrial cultures prohibit it. Who is to say which is right? It is the enormous undercurrent of this sort of relativism about what is right that supports the pluralism about the good that is so indicative of the liberal political framework. It is a relativism that is increasingly coming under attack in contemporary life, if not always for the best reasons.[1]

Note that I label the second problem the 'pluralism' problem, not the 'relativism' problem. This is because in solving these two problems I shall have to enforce a strict adherence to labelling that keeps separate issues separate.[2] We are now entering an area where clarity has not been in vogue. Indeed the two problems just sketched are often confused. To make clear that they are distinct issues, consider the following analogy, which will then lead us into the means for resolving these problems.

2. The scientific analogy: the objective and the real

Contrast the case of moral descriptions with our scientific descriptions of the world. There are two separate features of the descriptions of the world that the natural sciences provide,

---

[1] See Allan Bloom's savage indictment of relativism in *The Closing of the American Mind* (New York 1987, London 1988). Bloom attacks relativism in order to restore a traditional conservative value set. Needless to say, that is not my motive.

[2] For further enforcement see my 'On the way the world is independent of

both of which seem important to the idea of science as the paradigm of objective enquiry. The features are distinguishable.

The first is this: Science describes the world in a way that is independent of the world's disposition to affect us in any particular way. A scientific description of the world is what we might call an *absolute* description. That is, it does not describe the world *relative* to any particular standpoint. Whatever cognitive apparatus a creature may bring to bear on the world (consider the possibility of creatures with radically different perceptual systems from the human kind), whatever interests and appetites other creatures may have, surely they would still be in a position to agree with us on the scientific descriptions. They would still agree with us on the mechanics of the world: round balls get stuck in square holes, spheres roll when placed on an inclined plane, etc. We might capture this feature of scientific descriptions, their *absoluteness*, thus: the applicability of a scientific description is accessible to all creatures no matter what perceptual systems, interests etc, they may have. More exactly:

> (1) A description *d* is absolute if and only if a creature *c* of any biological kind whatsoever could, without amending its biological nature, come to be suitably placed to assess the truth or falsity of *d*.

If a description does not satisfy (1) I will say that it is a *relative* description. The commonest example of a relative description is one using colour vocabulary, for many creatures could not be suitably placed to judge of the truth or falsity of the claim that tomatoes are red; they are simply not equipped to make the judgment. In contrast, to judge that a sphere rolls on an inclined plane it matters not at all what kind of perceptual system a creature has. It seems plausible to think that just so long as a creature has some sort of perceptual contact with the world it could be suitably placed to judge the truth of that remark.

The second feature of the natural sciences that impresses

---

the way we take it to be', *Inquiry* (1989) from which I draw in the following argument.

their importance as paradigmatically objective areas of enquiry is this: Our sciences exhibit *convergence*. What that means is that in science we work with the idea that there is such a thing as the truth towards which our enquiries are converging. We may not be sure how to measure this convergence and we may not be sure that we will be able to tell when, if ever, we achieve it, but it is a methodological constraint on our scientific activities that we expect our enquiries to converge. Of course, at any point in time there may be many different research avenues being explored on a given problem: for example, the identification and eradication of a particular virus. But, at the end of the day, we expect only one of these avenues to be the right one, unless, that is, we build together a picture that includes different approaches as commensurable but differing angles on a common theme. The central point to this aspect of scientific enquiry is that we expect that, for any given question, there is only one right answer. More exactly:

(2) For any proposition P the question 'Is it the case that P?' has only one right answer, 'Yes' or 'No'.

In science we expect our enquiries to converge on that answer.

Now absoluteness and convergence are different virtues of the scientific enterprise. This point can be overlooked for the following reason. The idea of convergence, which is the idea of *converging on the truth*, can be confused with the idea of agreement that arises when we employ such bare descriptions of the world that all creatures can come to agree on their applicability. But that idea, employing the importance of absolute descriptions, is a distinct idea. At best we might say that it invokes a notion of *convergence on a kind of description* of the world. This is agreement that arises when we shed our differences and agree on a suitable scale, a suitable way of describing the world, perhaps with absolute descriptions. But this is only agreement on the language, the descriptions to use in searching for the truth. However, the virtue of convergence is a matter of converging on the truth, not converging on a particular mode of description of the truth or falsity. It is important that we keep these things apart. Although in the natural sciences it is usual, before attempting to converge on the truth, to converge first on an absolute mode of description that is neutral with regard to our particular sensibilities and perceptual skills, the matters are logically distinct. The following example should seal the point.

Suppose we have two differing systems of description of the world that offer descriptions d_1 and d_2. Suppose d_1 employs normal human colour vocabulary and d_2 employs some radically different vocabulary peculiar to a species with very different perceptual systems to ours, call them Martians if you like. These descriptions, d_1 and d_2, are relative descriptions, for they do not satisfy definition (1). We cannot be placed to judge of the truth or falsity of d_2 and Martians cannot be placed to judge of the truth or falsity of d_1. We are each ineluctably incapable of knowing just what the other is talking about. Nevertheless both descriptions could satisfy definition (2), and the reason is simply this: the questions 'Is it the case that d_1?' and 'Is it the case that d_2?' are *different questions*. There might be only one right answer to the former and only one right answer to the latter, but because they are addressed in different vocabularies the answer to one has no bearing on the answer to the other. *There is room for both questions to have an answer.*

It follows from this that the truth about the world which stands as the goal of our convergence might turn out not to be expressible within just one agreed vocabulary. That is, the truth, that to which we try to converge, may require more than the limited vocabulary of absolute descriptions in order to be expressed. Converging on the truth is a different goal to reaching a common mode of description by, for example, restricting our descriptions of the world to absolute descriptions. There are more things in the world than are allowed for within the restrictive vocabulary of the natural sciences. *That,* at any rate, is the claim I shall now make use of.

The two features of the scientific enquiry that stand witness to its excellence enable us to draw a distinction between what is *real* and what is *objective*. Something is *real* if it can be located within the causal order of things within space and time that causally connect with one another. For the purposes of the present argument I propose that if something can figure in an absolute description of the world that is true, it is real. Note that this is not to identify being real with being capable of being given an absolute description, but the exceptions which, I think, rule out that identification are not pertinent to our present concern.[1] For the purposes of the present argument I shall ignore these exceptions.

In contrast, something is *objective* if and only if a description of it figures in a proposition which is true. That is, something is objective if there is some truth about it to which we might hope to converge. For example, numbers are objective but not real. The number two is an object in just the sense that there are truths about it to which we converge, like 'Twice two is four', and 'Two is half the square root of sixteen', etc. But the number two is not real. It is no good looking around the world and the things within the causal realm and expecting to bump into the number two. Sane people do not do that sort of thing, and they are right not to.

The short point to this distinction is this: Objectivity is a semantic concept, reality is a metaphysical concept. Applied to propositions, or to areas of discourse we may say:

(3) A proposition or discourse is objective if and only if there is a truth predicate for it,

and

(4) A proposition or discourse is real if and only if it employs only absolute vocabulary.

And now here comes the sticky question. When we ask questions like 'What is there?', meaning 'What sorts of things exist?', do we mean 'What things are real?', or 'What things are objects, or objective?'? It can seem pretty obvious to many people that the correct way of taking the 'What is there?' question is as a question about reality, but why? It seems a common assumption in our culture to take the natural sciences as the benchmark for what there is, so that if you cannot locate

[1] The main exception is the case of mental phenomena which, I believe, cannot be described in absolute terms but which, nevertheless, can engage in causal connections with other parts of the world. Both these claims are highly contentious. Materialists refuse to accept that mental phenomena cannot be captured within the language of the natural sciences, and certain sorts of mentalists refuse to allow mental events within causal relations. I think both are wrong, but that is all another story.

something with the causal machinery of scientific technology, it ain't there. But that is blind prejudice. For sure, there are many things that do not, and cannot, figure within the scientific view of the world, but that is just to say that they do not figure *within the world as described with the limited vocabulary of the natural sciences.* Clearly it does not follow from that that such things do not figure in the world. It all depends on whether we are willing to restrict our account of what there is to an account of what there is as described in a certain limited manner. I am not willing to do this, for I see no argument to say that we should.[1]

3. The moral hum of the world

Many people think that the idea that values could be objective is silly. They think values are subjective because they are relative. To say that an action is good is to describe it relative to the point of view of an emotionally sensitised human being; it is not to describe it as it is in itself. Morality and values in general are features of the way in which *we* react to, or perceive, the world which, considered in itself, is silent with respect to good and bad, right and wrong. This is the view of the moral silence of the world. The world is morally inert, the sound of values arises only within our own breasts as, creatures of passion that we are, we respond to the world. As an argument against the objectivity of values this has become known as the argument about the queerness of moral values.[2] It is not a good argument. In the light of the previous section the argument is easily met.

To sustain the moral hum of the world, the thought that values are objective, we need only substantiate the thought that evaluative utterances are subject to truth and falsity; they satisfy definition (3) above, that is all. The world as described by science, as described absolutely, is, of course, morally inert. But that is only to press the point that the moral hum of the world cannot be detected with a microphone! You need a human receiver to pick up the moral cacophony that abounds

[1] See my 'On the way the world is independent of the way we take it to be', op. cit., for more diagnosis of this point.
[2] Labelled such by John Mackie in his influential subjectivist tract, *Ethics: inventing right and wrong* (London 1978).

in our world. And that commits us to saying that moral utterances are relative; but that is okay, and, I think, probably true. But the moral of the last section was that whether or not an utterance is objective is independent of whether or not it is absolute. The two things are different.

Many philosophers recently have become impressed with the idea that an analogy between values and secondary qualities (like colours) is a useful way of supporting the objectivity of values. I think the analogy is precarious. There are many important differences between the two kinds of description. But this much is worth saying: *both descriptions are relative descriptions and, as such, are not thereby debarred from being objective accounts of what there is.*[1]

I conclude then that the problem of the relativity of values is not a problem. The problem of pluralism is much more important. I shall turn to that now.

4. Reviewing the situation

I started this chapter by identifying two distinct problems that seem to arise in promoting the idea of the objectivity of our moral values. The former problem, the relativity problem, I have cast aside as a purely philosophical conundrum flowing from a mistaken metaphysical view about the proper constraints imposed upon an account of what there is. The fact that evaluative descriptions of the world are relative does not stop them being, for all that, descriptions of the world that are objectively true or false. However, acceptance of the relative nature of such descriptions can readily lead to a worry about *relativism*. This is a separate worry. It is the worry that our moral descriptions might be relative to incommensurable different backgrounds between which there is no rational choice. Let me clarify this. It is the plurality problem announced in §1.

First, if our moral descriptions are relative, what are they relative to? The answer is this: When we say, for example, that an action is kind, our evaluation is relative to the moral tradition from within which we view the world. I have stressed

---

[1] One of the key difficulties for an extensive analogy is that the relativity of secondary qualities is accountable in terms of the physiological basis of our means for detecting colour. No such basis looks plausible in the case of values.

the importance of our moral traditions in developing my account of socialism. It is our traditions which ground the relativity of our moral discourse. However, it takes little reflection to realise that although our traditions may be required as a ground for the relativity of our moral talk, they also threaten relativism if it turns out that there is an incommensurable plurality to such traditions. If my tradition enjoins me to condemn, say, euthanasia while yours enjoins you to condone it, which tradition is right? We may find that because of the complexities and differences of cultural backgrounds our traditions seem barely commensurable, we are not sure how to measure them one against another. But it is clear that, notwithstanding this, they are incompatible, for they sanction opposing actions from the two of us. If this plurality of standards of what is right and wrong cannot be overcome, then the relativity of our moral talk which, in itself, is no longer a problem threatens relativism about the truth for morality. And that is a problem. It is a profound problem, and one that must be overcome if the enterprise of this book is to survive. For the problem with this pluralism is that it threatens the possibility that our moral discourse might exhibit the convergence that I noted as an important feature of our notion of objective truth. I have argued that it does not matter if moral discourse does not exhibit the *absoluteness* of description characteristic of the natural sciences. That is not a requirement of objectivity. However, the potential for convergence on the truth is, I believe, a necessary characteristic of an objective enquiry. The potential pluralism of moral traditions threatens this convergence.

5. The presumption of objectivity

The key point that needs addressing now is this. If it is convergence that matters for our notion of objective truth, any candidate for truth must satisfy (2) above, which was the requirement that,

> For any proposition P, the question – Is it the case that P?
> – has only one right answer.

It does not matter what vocabulary the question is framed in. In particular, it does not matter if the vocabulary is intelligible only from the vantage point of some human moral tradition. What does matter is that there should be just one right answer to any moral question we pose. It is this uniqueness of right answer that is threatened by pluralism.

But we must be clear what this idea of a unique right answer amounts to and, more important, what it does not. Acceptance of the idea for our morals and politics does not entail that political arguments are capable of solution in a way that is rationally incontrovertible. All that is entailed is that however difficult and complex the practice of political argumentation may be, there is a right answer to be had. The presumption of objectivity does not offer guidance on how we are to pick out the objectively right answers. The presumption is a metaphysical assumption, not an epistemological one. After all, about the only area of human enquiry where we think that objectively right answers are available through methods which reveal their correctness to be rationally incontrovertible is mathematics. Our normal empirical enquiries, including the natural sciences, although due a presumption of objectivity, are not areas in which the correctness of a view can be so rigorously defended. But, for all that, the correct view, if it is correct, is the right answer. Similarly, all that is required in assuming that our morals are objective is that, if a given answer is correct, its being correct is an objective matter of fact. As such, this presumption of objectivity does not help us to detect the right answers.

Someone might argue that there is no presumption of objectivity in our moral and political practices. I think that is wrong. It is, I believe, the one substantial assumption of my argument that our moral practices exhibit a presumption of objectivity. We engage in moral and political argument assuming that there are right answers to be had. I shall not argue for this point. I find it hard to account for the importance of our moral lives if we do not accept that we work under this presumption. That, it seems to me, is simply how things are for us in our moral lives. What I am trying to argue for is a way of doing justice to that presumption of objectivity. And to do that, we have to meet the threatened pluralism.

6. Weber: the gods and demons of value pluralism

The following seems a legitimate demand when someone

proffers an evaluation of an agent or action as good or bad. The demand is that they be able to give some reason in support of their view. The demand is legitimate because it arises for all assertions that make a claim of knowledge about the world. However, it is not possible that all the reasons we give in support of an evaluation are themselves subject to further support. At some point we seem to reach bedrock. Our chain of supporting reasons grounds in something we find self-evident or, perhaps, in an article of faith or commitment. Eventually we reach a belief that cannot itself be supported by further reasons.

This idea of bedrock beliefs is perfectly general and is not, in itself, a matter of concern. It is plausible to characterise part of the philosophical enterprise as an attempt to demarcate those beliefs in our conceptual scheme that have this foundational role. For example, we are now familiar with the idea that in attempting to prove the existence of the external world we reach bedrock with beliefs which admit no further justification and about which we can only say, 'This is how things are with me.' Such bedrock beliefs are the hinges about which our processes of justification and support turn.

Now this idea of bedrock beliefs is harmless as long as the beliefs that have this status are ones of sufficient generality to make them universally accepted. For example, likely candidates for the bedrock beliefs would be: belief in causation, belief in the existence of the spatio-temporal framework, belief in induction. These beliefs are harmlessly bedrock in so far as they are prerequisites for any rational thought. In our moral discourse things seem different.

It often appears to be like this. We have a moral disagreement, and when the disputants start to justify their positions they find that their chains of justification lead them to different and incompatible bedrock beliefs. Unlike the central metaphysical cases involving causation and the external world where, we hope, our chains of justification lead to one bedrock, in morals there appears to be a plurality of bedrocks the choice between which is abitrary or, at least, not susceptible of rational justification.

The thought then is that with our moral arguments we eventually reach a point where our acceptance of the bedrock beliefs is a matter of pre-rational choice, commitment, an article of faith, or something we simply find self-evident. We reach a level of beliefs expressive of ends and values which are taken as intrinsically good and which cannot be further defended or justified. This is the level where the agent must make a free choice of the basic ends and goods which give the contours to her moral experience as a whole. Such a choice is not made from within the content of her moral system, it is a choice which defines her moral system. And if the apparent plurality of such basic choices cannot be overcome, relativism ensues and there is no objective truth predicate available for our moral and political discourse.

Something like the above account of why there is such a problem about objectivity for morals and politics and why the moral hum of the world thesis looks false is to be found in much twentieth-century moral philosophy. Its definitive statement appears in the work of Max Weber. Weber unerringly gives expression to the thesis of the moral silence of the world. In so far as we have, as a culture, come to accept this silence, his description of the predominant western political culture as structured by what he calls the 'ethical irrationality of the world' is disturbingly accurate.[1]

Weber distinguishes between *formal* and *substantive* rationality. The former refers to the calculability of means and procedures, the latter to the value of ends from some point of view. It is important that substantive rationality is relative to some point of view, for it is central to Weber's account of modern society that rationality does not inhere in things themselves but is always ascribed to them by an agent or agents. Rationality is thus a relative concept; only from a certain point of view can we say that a thing is rational or irrational.[2]

With regard to formal rationality modern society, specifically capitalism, is highly rational in so far as it permits and encourages the maximising of the calculability of action. This is also true of science and the modern legal and administrative

[1] *From Max Weber: essays in sociology*, translated and edited by Gerth & Mills (New York 1946), 122. I am indebted to Roger Brubaker's excellent little book, *The Limits of Rationality* (London 1984) for much of the discussion of Weber here.

[2] *The Protestant Ethic and the Spirit of Capitalism*, 194 n. 4, 'a thing is never irrational in itself, but only from a particular point of view. For the unbeliever every religious way of life is irrational, for the hedonist every ascetic standard.'

systems. However, with regard to questions of substantive rationality, modern society is helpless, for here we can only evaluate the formal rationality of some institution with regard to the ends and values already chosen. With regard to the ends and values themselves the rationality of modern society is neutral. As Brubaker notes, 'it is this substantive neutrality, this indifference to all substantive ends and values, that makes the rationality of the modern Western social order "specific and peculiar"'.[1] It is this characterisation of the modern social order, the way in which it supports the interminable conflicts between the 'Gods and Demons' of different value orientations which is so central to the modern predicament.[2] According to Weber, values are essentially subjective. This is in contrast to the scientific account of the world which is objective and which fuels the applicability of formal rationality. Science gives us the means for enhancing the calculability of action ordered with respect to some chosen end or value, but it does not deliver procedures for choosing such ends or values. Questions as to how conflicts between 'several concretely conflicting ends are to be arbitrated are entirely matters of *choice or compromise*. There is no scientific procedure of any kind whatsoever which can provide us with a decision here.'[3] Whereas scientific truth is what is valid for all who seek the truth, value orientations are subjective: 'We cannot learn the *meaning* of the world from the results of its analysis.'[4] The thesis of the moral silence of the world is explicit in Weber:[5]

> As intellectualism suppresses belief in magic, the world's processes become disenchanted, lose their magical significance, and henceforth simply 'are' and 'happen' but no longer signify anything.

The disenchantment of the world brought on by the advance of science reveals the evaluative barrenness of the world and so values have to be created in each individual's ultimate choice of basic ends and values.

[1] Op. cit., 38.
[2] See *From Max Weber*, op. cit., 148 for the 'gods and demons'.
[3] *The Methodology of the Social Sciences*, translated and edited by Shils & Finch (New York 1949), 18-19.
[4] Ibid., 57.
[5] *Economy and Society*, 506.

7. Repairing the disenchantment of the world

Within Weber's diagnosis of the modern world we can detect
both problems announced at the beginning of this chapter: the
relativity problem and the pluralism problem. Given the
argument so far I simply do not think that the relativity of our
moral and political discourse is a problem. That is not enough
to warrant the moral disenchantment of the world. The moral
silence of the world is pressed by the pluralism problem; it is
that which prompts our disenchantment.

We have to solve the pluralism problem. Let me make a few
remarks on the general character of the solution that I shall
offer. As the problem is set up it appears to be insoluble. For if,
from the vantage point of tradition T_1 I applaud an action
which, from the vantage point of tradition T_2, you condemn,
there looks to be no ground from which we might adjudicate
the dispute. This is because I have stressed the foundational
role of our traditions to our moral and political life. The
traditions we learn and apply within our reference groups
shape our moral experience. They ground those experiences,
and therefore we cannot step outside these traditions in order
to adjudicate disputes that arise between traditions. This looks
to leave it that we can only have moral arguments with our
close neighbours; with those more distant we can only fight.
That is not a happy conclusion. However, given the stress I
have laid upon the concept of a tradition in grounding our
moral life, I am limited in my solution to the pluralism problem
by the following constraint: The solution must appeal to
structural features of moral discourse; it cannot appeal to the
content of the discourse. What I mean here is this.

The solution would appeal to the content of moral discourse
if it argued that the values of my tradition (or yours) were
correct in contrast to the values of your tradition (or mine).
That is, such a solution directly seeks a way of championing
one tradition against another. But that is simply not possible
given the foundational role that I am allowing to traditions.
However, by a solution that appeals to structural features of
moral discourse I mean a solution that identifies certain
general formal properties that our moral traditions must
exhibit on pain of failing to meet the presumption of
objectivity. The thought is then that if in a dispute one (or

both) traditions can be shown to fail on these formal properties then, although this does not show that its prescriptions are false, it does remove them from the catalogue of rationally defendable options. Intuitions of value made from within a tradition that fails such a structural test of fitness face a *prima facie* charge of distortion. We have reason to believe that such value claims are distorted. And that leaves the opponent, providing her tradition gets a clear licence, with a more supportable claim to have got at the moral truth. Of course nothing is ever finally settled in such disputes, but that is true of our scientific enquiries too. What I shall now do is outline a charge of ideology which amounts to a structural criticism of moral traditions.

8. Sketch of a theory of ideology

What we need at this point is a notion of a practice of reflection, a way of arguing that enables us to criticise our traditions. But the reflective practice we seek is not one that enables us to stand outside our traditions and criticise them from some Archimedean point of view. It is a practice of critique that is intrinsic to any tradition.

A first outline sketch of the abstract nature of the required notion of critique goes like this. Suppose that, *ceteris paribus*, our moral intuitions are *bona fide* cognitive claims licensed *sui generis*. We then need to show that, when things are not equal, their licence is ripe for withdrawal.

The simple idea behind the concept of a distorted intuition that I want to develop is this: A distorted intuition of some value is one such that *the only explanation we could have for someone's intuiting that value is that adherence to the value serves some function in the economic arrangement of their society*. The idea is that in so far as we do justice to the presumption of objectivity our intuitions of value must be supportable by the provision of reasons. This is a limited point. It requires no more than that there should be some web of beliefs in which we locate an intuition. However, a constraint on this web of belief is that it should not be *closed*. What this means is that the web of belief is closed if and only if for any particular intuition within the web there is only a circular defence of the belief available. The requirement of non-closure is not enforceable all the time; it becomes pressing only when our traditions conflict.

What I have to do is to define the notion of the closure of a system of beliefs and how, when the closure condition arises, otherwise cognitive claims made from with the system are no longer credibly defended as *sui generis* reasonable. The *ceteris paribus* clause in defence of the autonomy of the intuitions is then that our moral beliefs should not exhibit closure under times of conflict.

Having clarified the concept of closure, and this is a purely metaphysical task, I shall then show how the concept applies to systems of moral beliefs. In doing that I shall assume that the usual cause of closure is economic. This is the Marxist insight that perceived values are a function of economic interest. For Marx, it seems that this claim was applied *tout court* to all morality. I am not supporting that idea. The idea that I am extracting from Marx is simply this: By employing the concept of closure we demarcate those cases where a perceived value is shown to be the result of a distorted intuition, where the distortion is caused by economic interests.[1] Economic factors can distort our perceptions of value. That is the claim that I shall develop in order to provide a concept of critique that does justice both to the foundational role of our traditions and the presumption of objectivity.

Of course, in doing this I am open to the stock charge that such attempts to connect explanation of the causes of moral beliefs and the assessment of those beliefs falls foul of the genetic and naturalistic fallacies. Although I think these charges are often employed in too ready a manner in moral philosophy as stock-in-trade trump cards, it is not enough in reply to the purists to say, 'So much the worse for your

---

[1] In not accepting the *tout court* claim that Morality is Ideological I see no reason to accept Lukes' claim that there is a paradox in Marxism about the place of values, cf. S. Lukes, *Marxism and Morality* (Oxford 1984). Lukes' paradox concerns the co-tenability of the general claim and Marx's many evaluative denunciations of capitalism. The limited version of the 'morality is ideological' claim with which I am working allows that some morality is ideological but some is not; it will depend on which parts are distorted. It may just turn out that those values Marx appealed to in criticising capitalism are the undistorted ones. But I am not too concerned with the exegetical question of what Marx meant on all this; the important question is what we might mean.

fallacies.' Making the connection between explanation and assessment is not straightforward, but the account I give will accommodate these charges of fallacy.

To honour the promises just made, let me introduce the kind of example where the concept of critique I am interested in seems applicable. Take the case of a moral tradition considered as a codification of an agent's point of view: for example, the tradition of white South Africans. Of course, any codification of an agent's beliefs is problematic; for, for the agent, her moral outlook is usually unreflective. The codification required is not, however, an obstacle to the analysis, for it is employed, not as a representation of the agent's moral phenomenology, but in order to bring out the structural property of belief systems that I call closure.[1] Having defined closure I shall then suggest how functional explanations can be employed to explain away certain moral traditions. Note, this is not a general claim. It is not a vulgar Marxism that explains all morality as a function of class interest. Rather, I shall demarcate special cases in which the explaining away is licit. These are cases of closure. They have the following general characteristics.

We have some community C which possesses a tradition T; for example, white South Africans and the tradition of apartheid. Suppose we have a candidate explanation E of the form,

C hold T because ...

where the dots are to be filled by some more or less sophisticated account of C's economic interests. T could be functionally explained in terms of, say, economic superiority for C. Furthermore T's function is sufficiently well correlated with economic superiority to make plausible its explanatory power in E. Further there is an explanatory puzzlement about T.[2] This seems to be the case with apartheid. There is an

---

[1] Of course I am here passing over complicated and large issues concerning the viability of the concept of false-consciousness, but much proof is in the pudding and space does not permit the detour.

[2] I follow Gerry Cohen for an account of functional explanations, see his *Karl Marx's Theory of History: a defence* (Oxford 1977), esp. chs. 9, 10. Cohen has come in for a lot of criticism, most of it misdirected. See especially the running debate with Jon Elster: Elster, 'Marxism, functionalism and game theory', *Theory and Society* (1982); Cohen, 'Functional explanation, consequence

explanatory puzzlement about how and why such a system of beliefs came into being and persists. The worry in such a case is to make this puzzlement clearly articulated. It is here that much work still needs to be done. However, even granted all these provisos, and they are large, why should we think E plays any role in our moral evaluation of apartheid? The answer I wish to press is this: E has a role to play if the following condition is met. The condition is that the tradition T is *closed*.

A closed tradition is one with the following structural characteristics. It is a tradition T such that C's defence or justification of events using T proceeds through the giving of reasons $r_1 \ldots r_n$ where the fact that these reasons are thought relevant is due to some central assumption(s) R which is paradigmatic or constitutive of the sorts of reasons $r_1 \ldots r_n$ proffered in support of T, and where R is not defendable in a non-circular example. For example, take a non-moral tradition, where T is a scientific theory, say Newtonian mechanics. In this case R will include the proposition that the mass of an object is an invariant. Or, to take a different moral case, if T is the moral tradition of the bourgeoisie R will include a claim about the inviolability of property rights.

The problem of closure is now this. When an R can stand in no pattern of justification or defence we have reached rock bottom. With the South Africans we reach rock bottom when we come to the belief that racial identity is a morally relevant factor in the determination of action. This is where their tradition comes to rest, in a belief that forms the most basic and general contours of their moral life. With such cases, we would first have to accept the appropriate R before we could see any point in the reasons C give for their beliefs. With such

---

explanation and marxism', *Inquiry* (1982); Elster, *Making Sense of Marx* (Cambridge 1985). Generally, Elster swipes at Cohen for uses of functional explanation that Cohen would also condemn, but his advocacy of methodological individualism leaves an area of disagreement between the two. The requirement in the text that there be an explanatory puzzlement about T is meant to address this point. Methodological individualists miss the way that we can be puzzled about some social object *qua* social object. Such is the case with apartheid. However, I do not wish to get embroiled here in the details of the controversy over functional explanations. Suffice to note that if the concept cannot be got to work, so much the worse for the present enterprise. However, I share Cohen's optimism that functional explanations are all right.

central beliefs, the agents can go no further in defending their views without their opponent's first accepting the relevant R. But, in that case, acceptance of R is not a cognitive act, something for which there is a reason. It is an act of faith: more often, simply conditioning. It is in such situations that we have characteristic metaphysical disputes in the pejorative sense of that adjective. Conversely it is definitive of genuinely cognitive pursuits that we do not reach rock-bottom in this way, that the pursuit for reasons proceeds unhindered.

Of course the idea that we must eventually reach rock-bottom in our beliefs is familiar and probably true. But, as noted above, when Wittgenstein spoke of our reaching rock-bottom with 'hinge beliefs'[1] this concerned high-level beliefs about induction, belief in the existence of the external world, an objective temporal order, etc. That such beliefs turn out to be rock-bottom and thereby unjustifiable does not matter, for the 'tradition of thought' characterised by these is, arguably, universal. It is the tradition of thought of the transcendental 'we'. This is not the case in the examples I am discussing.

The difference here might be put like this. The closure of beliefs in the tradition of the transcendental 'we' is *semantic closure*. We reach rock bottom in our justifications with the beliefs that fascinated Wittgenstein because of the very meaning of the concepts involved. It is reasonable to think that such concepts have to be basic to any system of rational thought. The kind of closure I am criticising in moral traditions is, however, *pragmatic closure*; the closure is a function of the attitude of the agents. The point of the criticism is, if you like, the agents' tendency to ossify their presumed cognitive beliefs into semantically closed traditions: they turn their supposedly cognitive claims of morals into metaphysics.

I shall not argue here for the identification of genuinely cognitive pursuits with the absence of closure in our belief systems, for I think it has sufficient *prima facie* plausibility to excuse such argument now. However, in order that this point should be noted for the role it is playing in the argument, let us accord it the status of a principle and note it as:[2]

---

[1] *On Certainty* (Oxford 1969), sections 341, 343.

[2] See my *Language, Logic and Experience* (London 1988) for more on these themes and their relation to issues concerning the justification of logic and realism and anti-realism.

Principle *K*: Genuine cognitive claims are in principle open to rational, non-circular, defence.

The point of something like an explanation of the apartheid tradition is now this. If *R* is meant to be a genuine cognitive claim, it should, in principle, be susceptible of rational defence by the giving of reasons that are non-circular. But *R* is not open to such defence. So we have the following disjunctive challenge to *C*: Either provide support for *R* – engage in rational non-circular enquiry in its defence – or we conclude that *R*'s preponderance in *C* is not due to its being a *bona fide* cognitive claim, but solely to its performing the functional role identified by *E*. That is, *C* do not believe *R* (and hence also *T*) because it is true, or even that they have good reason for believing it; they believe it because (causal) it serves a certain functional role. It is because of the prevailing economic arrangement of their society that *C* believe *R* and *T*; they do not hold it true for any rational reason.

In itself this does not show that *R* is *false*. It only shows that it lacks the credential for survival as a rationally defendable evaluative belief. But this is enough to operate as a filter and charge that the intuitions of value generated within *T* which give rise to conflict are distorted and are thereby to be filtered out. The connection of the functional explanation of *T* for *C* with the evaluative denunciation of *T* is that of a corrective filter to mark out those intuitions that are not embedded within a tradition that is in principle open. The requirement that the tradition be open is the requirement pressed by the presumption of objectivity, and it is this that is captured in principle *K*.

9. Morality and the angels

The notion of critique is a dynamic concept of critique. Further, it is a dynamic which has no need of a goal towards which the process is heading. This is important. The above account might be easily misunderstood in the following manner. Let me introduce the concept of an angel. I shall define an angel as:

Angel =$_{df}$ one whose moral outlook is derived purely from reason alone.

That is, one thinks of the angel as one whose moral outlook is wholly unaffected by economic or other factors which can distort the moral outlooks of mortals. Now the dynamic I have in mind is not one that is fuelled by a teleology aimed at turning us into angels. For one thing it is totally unclear what could fuel such a teleology other than a highly contentious account of the end of human life. We would first have to solve all our moral conundrums before we could characterise the end, the *telos* that fuelled the critique. Further, I doubt that angels could be moral if their behaviour were not in any way affected by their emotional appetites, or if they had no appetites at all.

The point of the preceding outline is to suggest that the dynamic is simply one of removing the closure conditions on our moral traditions without any conception of there being an end state to which the dynamic aims. This is in contrast to, say, Habermas's notion of a dynamic of critique aimed at arriving at a fully and rationally open or just communicative dialogue between agents. My dynamic is defined wholly in terms of where it is going from, not where it is going to. Put this another way. The critique aims to provide a background that is in principle open, but the point of the critique is not defined in terms of the terminus, if indeed there is one. The point is that we meet the presumption of objectivity by engaging in the practice of such a critique as outlined. It is the activity of critique that matters, not a quasi-utopian vision of the terminus. That is why the account of socialism on offer in this book is a second-order socialism, not TB socialism.

10. An analogy

Let me give an analogy to bring down to earth the highly abstract discussion so far. Consider the rise of modern science in the European Enlightenment, and consider the case of a discussion between two physicists, one a believer in medieval impetus mechanics and the other an advocate of the new experimental modes of reasoning. The medieval would argue his case by producing authorities, the reverential texts in terms of which everything is to be explained. The modern argues with regard to experimental data.

Now we can take as an analogy with the proposed dynamic of

moral and political tradition emendation the following task. Suppose a monk given over to the modern way of thinking were to go through all the current tracts of celestial mechanics. He takes each book in turn and identifies the central axioms and theorems upon which the book is based. He then asks whether there is any reason to believe these propositions other than that they have been passed down by authority. When there is no further reason he refuses to enter them in his book called *What we might Know about Celestial Mechanics*. Only those propositions of the various theories he investigates that have some experimental data in non-circular support of them find their way into his book. Even of these he cannot be sure that they are right – hence the 'might' in his title. Their licence to appear in his book is simply that they have survived experience and the critical investigation that looks to see if their previous acceptance was due only to authority.

In a similar way we engage in an objective and critical assessment of values when we turn to do for our value traditions as the monk does for his texts on mechanics. In cases of disagreement we look for the survivors in traditions, those evaluative beliefs that survive experience and the demand for rational defence, weeding out those contentious beliefs *the only explanation of their having been held* is that they play an identifiable functional role within the believer's society. Of course we are unlike the monk in that we cannot step back from our traditions and coolly evaluate them in the manner of the monk and his texts on mechanics. We engage in our enquiry from a position firmly embedded in a moral and political tradition. This need not stop us taking such a critical attitude to our values; it simply adds a further difficulty to moral life.

11. Two objections deflected

I shall conclude this account of the charge of ideology by meeting a couple of objections. It will be said that I have committed the genetic and naturalistic fallacies: that is, that I have confused questions about the genesis of values and questions about what *is* the case with questions about what *ought* to be the case. This is not so. It would be so if I had claimed that the functional explanation E showed that the distorted intuition was false, but I was careful not to claim that. There is a fallacy to be avoided here and I avoided it. The existence of an explanation E for some intuition or tradition of intuitions that leads to conflict provides us with a disjunctive challenge: Either the agent provides further reasons in support of the distorted intuition – the agent removes the closure in the system – or we conclude that E gives the best explanation for the agent's adherence to the intuition. And although this leaves it open that the intuition could still turn out correct, as things stand, we have no reason to treat the intuition as a cognitive claim because it fails principle K. Further, if we have an explanation E, we have reason to treat it as a pathological condition. So we do not say that the intuition is false, only that the availability of the functional explanation *in the light of a failure to abide by principle K* is enough to take away the intuition's licence of cognitive fitness. For all that, it may turn out that a means will be found to return it to cognitive fitness.

Perhaps a more serious line of criticism would be this. It might be said that, on my account, we can have no quarrel with white South Africans about the *content* of their moral beliefs, only with the way that they are held. For the proposed critique operates not by attacking *what* they believe about blacks, but only for the fact that their beliefs are not organised into an open tradition. Whether or not a belief system is closed is not a semantic property of the system, but a pragmatic property concerned with the agent's attitude to the belief.[1] This objection is important. It raises again the point I made above that the sort of critique of traditions that I would offer would operate on structural features of traditions, not their content.

Of course in one sense we criticise white South Africans for the content of their beliefs in the sense that, psychologically, that is what impels us to argue with them. But this is only to say that their beliefs are unpalatable from our point of view. But I am prepared to accept that, in the important sense, we only criticise them for the structure of their belief system. This is a virtue. After all, bear in mind the possibility that they

---

[1] There are belief systems other than those of the transcendental 'we' where the closure is semantic. For example, it seems plausible to think that systems of religious belief are semantically closed. The lack of a non-circular justification for the existence of God is a function of the very meaning of the concept. Similar thoughts apply to regions of the transfinite. Cases of semantic closure are characteristic of traditional metaphysical disputes.

could turn out to be right. I am trying to do justice, not only to the foundational role of our traditions, but also to the presumption of objectivity. That being so, I want a notion of the rightness or wrongness of our moral intuitions that gives content to the idea that it is truth that matters in all this and not just subjective preferences. But if so, we ought in principle to accept the possibility that the racist might be right, regardless of how that thought strikes us. We need not believe this any more than we believe that there are fairies at the bottom of the garden. But just as, if I came across someone who believed that there were fairies at the bottom of the garden, I would not be able to say that that could be shown *a priori* to be wrong, given what we mean by 'fairies'; so too do I concede that we cannot show *a priori* that the racist is wrong. It is simply a confusion, which does none of us any good, to mistake a recognition of our fallibility for an expression of uncertainty. Our tradition might convince us that the racist is wrong, but the concept of a mistake should force us to acknowledge that we may be mistaken without shaking whatever convictions we have.

We can take the argument further. If some belief about the moral relevance of racial origins is a candidate for truth or falsity, the content of the belief had better not be what determines which truth value it has. It is the world that determines truth value, not content. The thought I am pressing is that, although we might have no direct and unassailable access to truth with moral propositions, we can approach truth through the structural concern for the removal of closure in our traditions. That is the best we can do, and it is not to suggest a lost chance of there having been a better way. For I think that that is also the best we can do in the natural sciences.

12. Conclusion

I have now suggested a model of critique for our moral traditions. It is a concept of critique which applies only when distortion, suggested by the occurrence of conflict, is diagnosed in our intuitions. We preserve the autonomy of our traditions, but also, because we have the idea of a critical theory of distortion, we preserve the presumption of objectivity central to our intuitively grasped practices. The critical theory operates by invoking a general demand on cognitive beliefs that they be members of open systems of beliefs. The concept of closure is not a semantic concept but a pragmatic one. Systems that are semantically closed produce the classically interminable debates of metaphysics. The drive to remove pragmatic closure is just the drive to keep our moral traditions within the compass of cognition, as fits the presumption of objectivity, and not to let them ossify into imitations of metaphysics.

If the argument of this chapter is right we can proceed to employ the concept of a tradition in the way I have suggested, for we have the apparatus to avoid the charge of relativism. In principle, I have defended the idea that our traditions might deliver us objective moral truths. Of course the practice of ideological critique of competing traditions will be complex and contentious. It has not been my intention to start that practice. My aim has only been to show that the practice is available and that, theoretically, the fundamental legitimation of socialist interference that I have proposed, by being founded on the concept of the good, is in turn genuinely supported by the concept of a tradition. In Chapter 5 I shall outline an ideological critique of a dominant concept of justice. However, in general, I must leave detailed critiques to another occasion. Getting the sorts of critique that I have suggested to work will involve much interdisciplinary work in identifying traditions and their closure conditions. For the moment I am content to show the possibility and desirability of doing this.[1]

---

[1] I hope to find the opportunity to develop this theory of critique and to employ it in the future.

4

Freedom and Choice

Without exception the single most frequently cited fear of socialism is the threat that it is held to embody to familiar and justly cherished freedoms. Indeed, so often is the debate about socialism put in terms of the attempt to perfect a fine balancing act between the goals of freedom and equality, that the need for socialists to advertise their credentials as advocates of liberty has become a millstone around their necks. The appropriateness of this high-wire spectacle has become an accepted part not only of the general collective consciousness but also of much theoretical discussion of socialism.[1] This is not good enough. As long as socialists continue to feel embarrassed into justifying a delicate balancing act, they have given away too much to the libertarian agenda in terms of which the threats to liberty are posed. We need to put the alternative agenda firmly in place. In this chapter I want to put freedom in its place within the theoretical framework I am developing for socialism.

1. Freedom and interference

This much is clear: A socialist government will act to limit the economic freedoms of the free market. We have always known that this will be the case. If the argument of the preceding chapters is right we have a reason why they should so act. The reason is this. Socialism is concerned with enabling the re-emergence of the reference groups that carry the traditions of thought and feeling necessary for the good life to flourish.

[1] For example, Bryan Gould's *Socialism and Freedom* (Basingstoke 1985), or Alan Ryan's 'Liberty and socialism' in *Fabian Essays in Socialist Thought*, ed. Ben Pimlott (London 1984).

The possibility of society being organised by the dictates of the Good, the possibility that we organise our institutions to bring about moral life in society (a civil society), requires that we inhibit the forces of capital that have dislocated our moral purpose.

More specifically the argument presses the thought that there are areas of our social life, aspects of our moral agency, which are defined by criteria of success that are independent of the criteria of economic success. In various different institutions and arenas of social agency we have need of goals and conceptions of goods that mark the proper aim of success. For example, success in the provision of education for our young is measured by standards the articulation of which still leaves much to be desired. Nevertheless there is a tradition, much buffeted by recent events, that holds that education is to do with instilling a critical inquiring attitude in our children along with the analytical and expressive resources to carry through criticism where required and to impart the results to others. Education is not, despite the superficial but often striking appearance, a matter of teaching a dog to jump through hoops. Mental gymnastics may have a role to play in instilling the appropriate analytical skills we wish our children to absorb, but they are a means to an end, not the end in itself. It is the short-sighted unawareness of the existence of ends beyond the means that marks the neanderthal destructiveness of the 1988 Education Reform Act. This is a piece of legislation which, in effect, goes a long way towards supplanting the standards appropriate to evaluating our education system with the measuring stick of market success in a school's ability to churn out a homogeneous vocationally trained workforce. It is a striking feature of the way the education reforms were elaborated that at no point in the consultation process was the opinion of educationalists sought. Analogous remarks apply to other areas of social life and other institutions, obvious ones being health-care provision and those service industries where it is plausible to think that the first priorities are servicing an essential need for a community, not making a profit – energy, water, communications. I shall employ these cases, as required, to exemplify my argument.

Now I have already argued[1] that if socialists are to employ a

---

[1] Chapter 1, §2.

concept of freedom in articulating their position it will have to be a notion of freedom that is dependent on an antecedent conception of the good. What I shall argue in this chapter is the following. *Any* coherent concept of freedom must be secondary to our being provided with the means and opportunity to articulate the criteria of goods and success appropriate to the various arenas of social life. For example, the freedom to chose which school our children go to only makes sense within a framework in which the criteria of success in education have some hope of being articulated. That is to say, the much vaunted freedom of choice is inapplicable if the choice is not one informed by the criteria of good appropriate to the particular domain. Choosing a school for one's children is a rational choice, something for which we hope there are standards to assess the choice as good or bad. The choice does not take place in a vacuum. But then this means that this freedom of choice can only exist where the traditions supplying the criteria are available. And that means that such traditions which supply the non-market criteria for evaluating educational provision must first be defended and protected from the intrusion of inappropriate criteria before the freedom of choice can have point or value. Such, in brief, is the course the argument of this chapter will take. Freedom is not an end in itself; it is only a means by which we partake of the traditions which supply our continually evolving criteria of the good in such matters as education, health and housing.

To put it another way: Socialists will interfere with the economic freedom capital requires for the efficient pursuit of profit so that the non-market criteria of goods may be encouraged and, in turn, provide the marks by which we then indulge in those freedoms of choice that are of profound importance to us in our social life. It is only when our liberties are protected within the compass of rich possibilities for the good life, within the framework of a civil society, that they are worth fighting for and championing, for it is only within such compass that, for example, a coherent content can be given to wanting the freedom to choose which school one's child goes to.

2. An historical interlude

At this point it would be foolish not to take note of a familiar and much employed distinction: the distinction between negative and positive freedom. Although I believe that the distinction is not without problems, given its familiarity, it is as good a background as any other from which to strike out the account of freedom and choice I wish to defend.

The notion of negative freedom, as Berlin put it, goes like this:[1]

> I am normally said to be free to the degree to which no man or body of men interferes with my activity. Political liberty in this sense is simply that area within which a man can act unobstructed by others.

This concept is to be contrasted with that of positive freedom the core of which is well captured by Berlin again:[2]

> The 'positive' sense of the word 'liberty' derives from the wish on the part of the individual to be his own master.

On the face of it it is not clear what the difference here is supposed to be. Both negative and positive freedom are concerned with claims against interference, and it has been argued that there is no real difference in concepts between the political traditions associated with the notions. The difference, so it has been claimed, is more a matter of what different political theorists have to say about the nature of the human subject who claims her liberty from interference.[3] While I suspect that this point is right and that Berlin was, strictly speaking, wrong to speak of two concepts, he did nevertheless express acutely the main difference in the account of human nature that underlies the differing traditions of negative and positive freedom.

The concept of positive freedom holds that the agent is free only when she is her own master and it is this idea of self-mastery that carries the seed of difference that marks positive freedom as something more than negative freedom.

---

[1] I. Berlin, 'Two concepts of liberty', reprinted in his *Four Essays on Liberty* (Oxford 1969), 122.

[2] Ibid., 131.

[3] The *locus classicus* for this argument is Macallum, 'Negative and positive freedom', *Philosophical Review* (1967), who points out that conceptually both negative and positive freedom are triadic relations between agents, constraints and ends; the difference in the two traditions amounts to differences in the accounts of these variables.

For once the idea of self-mastery becomes important we have to ask, 'From what and from whom must we be released from bondage in order to achieve self-mastery?' And it is the generality of this question that raises the possibility that there are more things in this world than other agents to which we can be in slavery. Most important of all, the possibility is raised that an agent can be a slave to herself, or to her passions, her lower nature, her misconceptions, etc. Positive freedom is still a matter of being free from various impediments; the difference is that it postulates a definite goal that such things impede, namely self-mastery. Further, if it is possible that an agent be a slave to her lower self or whatever, this goal is something that is in principle objectively described. And by that I mean to note this: the goal of self-mastery is not necessarily transparent to the subject. More briskly:

(1) The individual agent is not necessarily the best authority on the goal of positive freedom, self-mastery.

It is this claim that marks the boundary between negative and positive freedom. In effect this difference amounts to the following:

Positive freedom is a concern for freedom which is secondary to the goal of self-mastery; negative freedom is a concern for freedom as an end in itself.

And it is because the goal of self-mastery allows the possibility that others may be in a better position to see one's bondage than oneself that positive freedom appears to allow the idea of forcing an agent to be free.

It is this idea of 'forcing to be free' that rightly troubled Berlin in his essay. He quotes Fichte on this:[1]

To compel men to adopt the right form of government, to impose Right on them by force, is not only the right, but the sacred duty of every man who has both the insight and the power to do so.

Because the centrality of the idea of self-mastery invites the possibility that others can be as well if not better placed to know what would be in one's true interest, the concept of

[1] Quoted, op. cit., 151.

positive freedom makes freedom secondary to acting for one's own true interest – acting for the good. In contrast, negative freedom, in treating freedom as an end in itself has no room for the idea of the good. What matters first and foremost is not being interfered with, regardless of whether or not there is any notion of the good at all. Berlin is quite explicit on this, quoting Hobbes and Bentham approvingly, and notes that:[1]

> Law is a always a 'fetter', even if it protects you from being bound in chains that are heavier than those of the law, say, some more repressive law or custom, or arbitrary despotism or chaos.

Further, as Bentham said,[2]

> Is not liberty to do evil, liberty? If not, what is it?

In contrast, Berlin quotes the following claim made by a Jacobin club of Bentham's time:[3]

> No man is free in doing evil. To prevent him is to set him free.

The central concern to make the individual inviolable even from her own good is nowhere more clearly stated than in Berlin's championship of Bentham and Hobbes. For the theorist of negative freedom, being free from interference is in itself an end regardless of whether or not that interference offered is for the subject's good.

Clearly, in the light of the argument that I have been developing for socialism, with the concentration on the precedence of the good over concerns for rights, it would seem that any concept of freedom that can made to work within the position outlined will be more akin to positive freedom than negative freedom. This is right. This is what I meant when I said that freedom is secondary to our notion of the good, it does not take precedence. What I shall do now is this. First, I shall show that there is room for a position between the unrestricted negative freedoms of Hobbes and Bentham and the totalitarian

[1] Ibid., 123.
[2] Ibid., 148.
[3] Ibid.

employment of positive freedom found in Fichte. Acknowledging that freedom is secondary to some account of the good, whether in terms of self-mastery or not, does not entail the idea of 'forcing to be free'. Having shown the possibility of some such employment of the concept of positive freedom, I shall argue for its necessity.

3. Between Hobbes and Fichte

At root, the difference between the traditions of negative and positive freedom is this: For the former the subject has an undisputed authority over the question of what is in their own good, for the latter this is not so. That is why a subject's positive freedom can be realised by another agent acting so as to enable the subject to achieve self-mastery. The key issue is the authority of the subject. A simpler way of catching this point is to say that being negatively free is to enjoy an unrestricted choice of goods and goals, being positively free allows that the subject's choice of goods can be constrained by a conception of the good independent of the subject's recognition of those things as goods. In the former, negative sense, freedom consists in choosing goods where what is good is good because the subject chooses it. In the latter, positive sense, freedom consists in being able to acknowledge the good which is independent of one's choice. In short, *positive freedom arises when one is free from those things that inhibit one's deference to the authority of the good*. This brings out quite clearly the subservience of the concept of freedom to that of the good. Being free is still important, but it is not an unconstrained notion. What sorts of things agents need to be free from depends on what sorts of things count as goods. From the point of view of negative freedom, anything can count as a potential obstacle just so long as it inhibits an action that the agent chooses to undertake.

The scope for a position between Hobbes and Fichte should by now be apparent. The position is just this: freedom is held secondary to the concept of the good, the freedoms that matter are those that free us from obstacles that block or inhibit our deference to the authority of the good. However, although this is to break with the theorists of negative freedom, it is not to side with Fichte and to insist that it is legitimate to force someone to be free, to force them to show deference to the authority of the good. For it is precisely because the deference required under positive freedom is deference to the authority of the good that this marks a different option from one in which we are required to show deference to another agent. *That* can still be counted an infringement on our liberties, for it is still plausible to insist that a methodological requirement of deference to the authority of the good requires that no single agent or group of agents should assume, or be allowed to adopt, a position of master of the good. This is the point we met before in the Introduction, §4. Making freedom secondary to a deference to the authority of the good is a metaphysical point about the relative position of our political concepts in the logical geography of socialism. It is not to propose an epistemological thesis about who, if anyone, has the right to determine what the good is. And if we think that no one should be so privileged, it leaves it open that the appropriate methodology for genuine deference to the good requires that no one can legitimately force you to be free. Fichte's position is simply an irrelevance from the point of view of the coherence of a positive account of freedom.

So the position between Hobbes and Fichte is tenable. I shall now show why it has to be adopted. Following that, I shall expand the argument first sketched in §4 of the Introduction against the coherence of Fichte's position once we have adopted a positive notion of freedom. Taken together these arguments amount to a strong challenge to the liberal advocate of negative freedom who says, in effect, that both the negative theorist's priority of liberty over the good and the Fichtean extension of the positive theorist's position are incoherent. The only coherent position is the one just sketched and on offer in this essay.

4. Choice and criteria

Here is the central question that I want to consider: When we engage in choosing goods we make choices that are reasonable and are open to evaluation by various criteria; but which comes first, our choices or the criteria by which we assess them? We can flesh out this question in the following way.

There is a growing movement in contemporary society to give greater power to the consumer. The importance of consumer choice lies not only within the familiar efforts of consumer organisations concerned with product testing, it is rapidly becoming a key issue in our evaluation of public utilities and services. On both Right and Left, the importance of consumer choice has also become central to our evaluation of local government, and increasingly it has become a dominant theme in the articulation of policy at a national level.[1]

On the face of it, the attempt to adapt the consumer movement in the service of socialism looks to be a way of employing the language of negative liberty that makes it acceptable to socialists. I am sure many see it this way. But the consumerist approach to politics is broken-backed. On the Left it amounts to this. In many areas of social life, for example local government management of the roads, education and housing, there are non-market criteria of success. As consumer specialists will point out, consumers are as much if not more concerned with the quality of goods and services as with their cost. There is no mistaking the observation[2] that much of the demise of the British car industry in the seventies was due to the perceived poor quality of product regardless of the competitiveness of price. The consumerist approach for socialists then amounts to the idea that the Left should harness consumer power in promoting these non-market, non-profit-oriented goals. In so doing the Left will find a strong alliance between the desires of consumers to express choice over non-market goals and the desires of socialists to thwart the unfettered pursuit of profit. Promising though this thought may sound, I do not believe it is viable.

One objection to the consumerist approach, taken as our model of the centrality of the concept of choice, is this: It amounts to the sort of economism about values criticised in earlier chapters. The priority given to consumer choice, if unchecked, amounts to the sort of free-market in values criticised in Chapter 1 when we considered the position of the

---

[1] On the Right an obvious example is the centrality given to the notion of parent power in the government's Education Act, although there is some doubt about the extent of this power given the control the Act offers to central administration. On the Left, interest in consumers has come later but is now a vogue issue among sections of the British Labour Party. For example, see Martin Smith, *The Consumer Case for Socialism*, Fabian Society Pamphlet no. 513 (London 1986). Labour's 1988 policy review initiative included a group working on 'Consumers and the Public Sector' much informed by Smith's work.

[2] Cf. Smith, op. cit., 11.

market socialist.[1] But for the present I want to pursue a stronger argument against the centrality of choice unrestrained by the good, and I shall do so employing the consumer model.

If consumers are to make rational, reasonably defendable choices within the markets for goods (as also the markets for public utilities and services) there must be criteria that mark out what counts as a good choice. This is an obvious point, but it is often underplayed. For example, in the field of health care, those who advocate a voucher system whereby consumers can 'shop around' to get their operation done at the hospital of their choice often seem to think that an important desideratum in this choice is the length of operation waiting-lists at different hospitals. However, it takes little reflection to realise that this could well be a bad criterion for selecting a hospital. A hospital with short waiting-lists may be in that situation because the GPs who, under the *status quo*, refer patients to hospital have little faith in the ability of the surgeons at that hospital to do a good job. Now this shows that for effective choices to be made consumers must be in possession of much more information than is normally the case. But more than that, they must be in possession of *the right information*. Clearly, a patient who chooses her hospital on the basis of the colour of paint used on the front door of the institution is hardly making a rational choice. That is simply the wrong sort of consideration to take into account when, for example, choosing a hospital in which to have hip-replacement surgery.

In a similar vein, a large part of the hostility to the proposals embodied in the 1988 Education Act is due to the inadequacy of the criteria on which parents will be offered the chance to make the choice of school for their children. In short, there is a substantial question about what the appropriate non-market criteria are in many of the fields of our social and economic life in which we make choices about our consumption of goods and services. The point of my opening question can now be put like this: Should the suitability of the appropriate non-market criteria that guide our choices be itself something subject to consumer choice, or is this a matter antecedent to the

[1] Although originating with different personnel, the consumer socialist and the market socialist positions are clearly of a kind and are perceived to be so by their advocates.

operation of choice? I think the latter option is the only viable one, for if we thought the selection of the appropriate criteria was itself a matter of consumer choice we would be left with no criteria on which to make *that* choice. In that case, there is no rational choice and we might as well toss a coin, and that makes the choice about the sort of education provision we want for our children and the sort of health care we want altogether too flippant. These matters about what criteria are appropriate for assessing the consumer choices we make are matters of deadly seriousness.[1]

The general point behind the argument is this. Rational consumer choice does not and cannot take place within a vacuum. Such choice takes place within a structure, a framework of criteria, which enables the assessment of the choice as rational or not. However, for the framework of criteria to bite it cannot in turn be subject to consumer choice, for without a framework the notion of choice makes no sense. It would be a directionless commitment, not a choice. In short, consumerism is not viable with regard to the criteria which spell out the goals and standards of success for consumer choice. Where then do these various criteria come from? The only answer has to be this: *They come from the collaborative, collective enterprise of trying to trace the contours of the good.*

The nub of this argument is the idea that the consumer does not have ultimate sovereignty, indeed that she cannot have ultimate sovereignty. If she is to make rational choices, that implies that there are criteria, standards of aim, for those choices and these criteria provide the directedness of the choice. That being so, these criteria cannot themselves be subject to consumer choice. For rational consumer choice to work, the consumer must cede sovereignty to the only available source of the criteria of aim, the authority of the good as elaborated by our collective enterprise of assembling traditions of the good.

One reason why this is overlooked is that too often the

---

[1] Of course, the present government is well aware of this point. That is why, despite the rhetoric about parent power, they have emasculated parent choice within a centrally administered and highly constrained set of criteria. Note, in criticising *that* I am not shirking the need for criteria, merely noting the Fichte-type stance of the present government which implicitly claims an absolute access to the right criteria in the assessment of education provision.

consumerist case is put in terms of easy examples. For instance, it is relatively easy to agree with the plaint of the consumer against a local authority which fails to keep local roads in good order. But this is because the value of not having a series of pot-holes in your road is plain for all to see. In such a case, the appropriate criteria by which we might choose an alternative candidate in local government are pretty obvious. But in many arenas of social life, and certainly in the ones that matter most – education, health, housing – it is not so obvious what the appropriate criteria of choice are. Because of this, the situation can sometimes seem so indeterminate that we give up on the idea of there being any criteria of choice. But once we do that, we have given up on there being rational choice. For sure, in our current climate where, for example, proper informed discussion of the goals of education has been erased from the political agenda, it can seem appropriate to allow parent power unlimited freedom of choice. But doing so is a shirking of political responsibility. A government which refuses to canvass expert opinion and which refuses to allow proper debate about the goals of education is, perhaps, deceitful and manipulative, and deserving only of our contempt. But worse than that, it is a government that has shirked its responsibility to its citizens by thwarting the sort of dialogue and debate which alone can provide the traditions of good to guide our choices. In the important domains of social life, we need first to tackle the issue of the criteria of choice *before* we can sensibly take the consumerist stance.[1]

5. Choice: against Fichte

The only authority to which we should defer is the authority of the good. That being so we can never license the thought that we should force another to be free. The argument so far does not support totalitarianism. Indeed it is opposed to totalitarianism. To see how, we must first be clear what the Fichte threat is.

The worry is that in subjugating freedom to the authority of the good we might endorse the idea that we could legitimately

---

[1] At the time of writing the Labour Party review group on consumers and the public sector seems unable or unwilling to acknowledge this point.

force another to be free. By 'forcing to be free' I understand at
least the idea that we might impose values and beliefs upon
others. However, that is not quite enough. We need to
distinguish the sort of recommendation of values and
imposition that can legitimately take place and does take place
throughout our moral lives. In contrast, totalitarianism comes
about when a sort of tunnel vision of values is forced upon an
agent. This is not the case in those situations in which we
legitimately impose a resolution to some moral dilemma but
without thereby closing off all other frames of reference and
enquiry. Let us capture this contrast with an example.

Consider the instance of parents who wish to choose the best
school for their children, and compare the situation of parents
in two different cases. Let us call the first the 'Albanian model'.
In the Albanian model the parents are told that the
appropriate criteria for good schooling are x, y, z. Further, they
are told that no other criteria are appropriate and that
discussion of any other criteria is banned by whatever forces of
law are available to those who have laid down x, y, z as the
criteria for good education. Now, even if the parents in the
Albanian model get the chance to exercise choice on whether or
not a school satisfactorily meets x, y and z, this model still
embodies the idea of 'forcing to be free'. For the choice takes
place within the restricted tunnel-vision typical of totalitarian
regimes in which debate about the appropriateness of
state recommended criteria is stifled. For even if such parents
can choose by these criteria, their choice is forced down one
dimension of measurement. As a matter of fact, most
totalitarian regimes do not bother to allow choice once they
have fixed the only admissible dimension of evaluation, all
schools are assumed to supply x, y, and z with equal success.

Now contrast this with the second case, call it the 'Camelot
model'. In the Camelot model there is an open round-table
debate which, in principle, is never deemed to have finished.
However, at various stages in the debate, the participants have
to leave the table and act in the light of the decisions made so
far. In the Camelot model, our parents leave the table to make
their choice of schooling for their offspring. However, when
they come to do so they find that the state has laid down
certain criteria, x, y and z, that define the dimension of
evaluation. Indeed it might be as strong as this: The state

decrees that no school shall be allowed to operate that can not meet x, y and z to a specified degree. It seems to me that with one important proviso, the parents in the Camelot model have not been 'forced to be free'. The proviso is this: *The decision to implement criteria x, y and z as the appropriate criteria for good schooling was a decision arrived at under the conditions of the round-table debate.* For what the round-table debate provides is simply the format for our collaborative attempt to spell out the demands of the authority of the good. From time to time we may get it wrong. But as long as the results we employ in piecing together our civil traditions are not forced by the sort of tunnel-vision we get in the Albanian model, there is no legitimate complaint that we have been forced into a particular choice. Further, to protest at the results of the round-table debate amounts to no less than to want to disengage altogether from civil society, to break away and construct one's own debate on the good. Not only is this a particularly silly and pompous attitude to take, it is embryonic totalitarianism. For in disengaging from the round table, one sets up one's own notion of the good above the authority of that notion which is independent of any particular agent, the authority of the good we collectively strive to achieve. Any attempt at the breakaway good implicitly sets up the vision of some agent or group as better than that which depends on no particular agent at all.

Imposing a result about the good upon our society when that result has been sanctioned by the sort of round-table debate characteristic of the Camelot model is not forcing someone to be free. For although it may sometimes be thereby legitimate to impose a good upon an agent, there is no presumption that in so doing we are certain we are right or certain that we could not, in time, be shown to be mistaken. There is only the certainty that comes from having engaged in the sort of collaborative engagement with the good that is at the heart of the socialist perspective as I have been outlining it. If we take seriously our attempt to articulate the good life then not only is it extreme folly, but it is gross irresponsibility, not to act for that good when the occasion arises. More specifically, to engage in the process of trying to understand the educative process, of attempting to support and then follow the best research available into how children learn and fail, and of earnestly trying to learn from those whose experiences are at the centre of the educative process – teachers, educationalists, parents and children – to do all this and then fail to act upon the conceptions drawn from such study would be a gross dereliction of responsibility on the part of a democratically elected government. Having done all that, there is no rational, let alone moral, option left but to lay down the results of one's enquiries in terms of the prescribed criteria for schooling.

But the difference between this and the Albanian model is twofold. First, the criteria selected have come about in a certain way: namely, they arise out of a collaborative enterprise over which no one group or agent has overriding control. Secondly, given this, there is no guarantee that, when the parties of debate come to return to the round table to take up their deliberations they will not find a different resolution to a problem than the one previously acted upon. The enquiry is open-ended in terms both of how the results were arrived at and how the results will stand up to the passage of time. But acknowledging this should not enjoin us to the silence of inactivity when faced with the question of how to organise education for our children.

6. Two types of totalitarianism

In the light of the above argument I want to suggest that we can distinguish two types of totalitarianism. I think the distinction is useful in analysing our current predicament.

The first type I shall call 'simple totalitarianism'. This is the sort of regime which, by whatever forces it has at its disposal, imposes a particular conception of the good upon society. This is the tunnel-vision that comes from having a specific vision of the good imposed with no room left for criticism or the development of alternatives. Even if it were the case that the vision being promoted by such a regime was a vision that everyone would accept if given the opportunity to evaluate it, we rightly find it hard to approve of such action. The reason is simply this. Such totalitarianism infringes the independence of truth. It acts as if moral truth were something that it alone had access to and that is methodologically and metaphysically unsound, even if it so happens that the vision the regime promotes is the truth. There is a methodological requirement which we instinctively enforce that says that the truth should be accessible to all and be seen to be so. Only then do we have any epistemological hope that what is on offer is the truth. And it is because of this requirement that we applaud the Camelot model.

But consider this. There are more ways of infringing this methodological requirement and disrupting the Camelot model than by simply forcing a single vision upon a society. In particular, a regime can infringe this requirement and disrupt the Camelot model if it systematically acts so as to disable the workings of the Camelot-style debate. If a regime acts so as to stifle the authority of the good that arises from the proper working of the Camelot model, I suggest that it is a totalitarian regime of a more sophisticated and sinister kind.

For example, suppose a regime promotes institutions and economic structures in society that disable the Camelot tradition. For the Camelot debate to take place there are certain conditions of moral agency that have to be secured. A regime which systematically destroys the conditions of moral agency is a totalitarian regime, for it acquires a total control of social life not by supplanting genuine moral debate with a preferred vision of the good, but by emptying the only resources of critique. A nation can be subjugated by being forced, with the full panoply of secret police and armed militia, to accept a given creed as an unchallengeable article of faith. But a nation can be more fully subjugated and brought under total control when the devices of dissent and criticism are silenced and disabled, not by the brute heel of the jackboot, but by the emptiness of despair when our communities have been replaced with the fractured shells of civility which offer no comfort to isolated individuals.

When a regime acts to turn our social life into a pale shadow of the moral life, when a regime so encourages the economic forces of disruption which tear down our communities and traditions, with people left alone among the debris of the claimant union's building and the institutionalised squalor of the social security offices, then a regime acts in a grotesquely more effective version of totalitarianism. It is a totalitarianism which gives total contral of social life by emptying it of the very possibility of ever constructing the Camelot debate. Such a totalitarian regime deflates people. It deflates them not by the simple brute force of oppression, but by emptying social life of the conditions of citizenship.

If the argument of the preceding chapters is right, not only need we not fear the totalitarian charge of 'forcing to be free', and not only should we be bold in pressing our only authority as the authority of the good, but we should return the charge. For the inescapable conclusion of the argument must be this: In the UK, and nations like it, where the libertarian refusal to acknowledge the social dimension of the moral life has been put into effect in the service of capitalism, we live under a totalitarian regime. Whether or not it has been the explicit intention of the Thatcher government of the last ten years, it has acted so as systematically to empty social life of the traditions and community-carried norms that provide the only real framework for the Camelot debate. Mordred has run riot, and until the conditions for moral agency are returned the good life and the scope for free and rational choice are beyond our reach.

5

Justice, Equality and Citizenship

In the Introduction I employed examples concerning the notion
of social justice in order to draw out the centrality of the
concept of the good to familiar socialist themes. Since then I
have said nothing about justice. This may have been thought
surprising. For many people socialism is all about securing a
just distribution of goods and services in society. I shall now
argue that this is a mistake. I shall defend my lack of concern
for justice.

In a manner that should by now be becoming familiar I shall
argue that the concern for obtaining a just distribution of goods
and services ignores the way that the availability of certain
goods is a condition for entering full and active citizenship.
Therefore if the distribution of such goods is counted as
something to be bargained for or argued for, the argument for
socialism is already lost. For example, the distribution of
health, education and housing in society must first be settled
before we can ask questions about the justice of the
distribution of other goods. That is, such things are not in the
market for just or unjust distribution. They are not to be
counted as marketable goods about which questions of just
distribution are apposite. Money, motor cars and continental
holidays are things over which we might raise question of
distribution. They are *bona fide* goods for which there is an
issue whether a person's holdings in those goods is a just
holding. But the sorts of things the distribution of which
socialists typically care about are not of this kind. If a socialist
puts them into the melting pot of goods to be distributed the
argument is lost. The proper course is to insist that possession
of such goods is a necessary condition for moral agency and
citizenship. That is the argument that I shall pursue.

1. Why socialists appear to care about justice

Justice looks to be a central concern for socialists because most people confuse the question 'Is the distribution of goods in society just?' with the question 'Is the distribution of goods in society equal?' But these are distinct questions. For sure, it seems legitimate to think that the first amounts to 'Is the distribution of goods in society fair?', but it is not clear that the only tenable notion of a fair distribution is that of an equal distribution. These are different matters. Furthermore not only is an argument required in order to convert a concern for justice into a concern for equality, but I do not believe that there is a cogent argument available to do the trick. For most socialists that would be a thoroughly dispiriting thought, but it is not really. I shall substantiate that thought shortly. For now I want to clarify why the concern for justice misses what I have argued is central to socialism.

Suppose that the concern for justice is the same as a concern for equality of distribution of goods. That is, let us suppose that there is some abstract requirement, issuing from goodness knows where, that goods should be distributed equally in society and that this requirement is the cornerstone of socialism. Now, of course, this simply goes against all the argument offered so far for taking a concern to achieve the good life, lived under the authority of the good, as the central plank of socialism. But exactly why and at what point would the proposed central concern for equality of distribution cross the presumptions of my argument?

My main worry with the abstract demand for equality is this: it commits us to economism about values. The reason is that it treats those items adequate possession of which is a necessary condition for citizenship as too much part of a general market of goods the distribution of which is to be bargained for in one way or another. That is, there are certain goods possession of which amounts to an absolute need if an agent is to have any chance of achieving the good life. A person's need for such things does not arise from an abstract demand for a certain pattern of distribution, for example, an equal distribution. The need arises because without them she cannot attain moral agency; without them she will not be placed in a position to partake of the good life.

2. Primary and secondary goods

We need to mark a distinction between the different sorts of goods, the distribution of which poses such problems for political theory and practice. In the first place there are goods possession of which is a necessary condition for a person to achieve moral agency. In the second place, there are those goods the distribution of which does not affect the conditions of moral agency. We might express this by speaking of primary goods versus secondary goods, but by that I mean more than that the former are more important. That would not capture the importance of the first kind of goods. Similarly, simply to say that there are goods that people need, rather than merely desire, lacks some of the potency of the distinction I wish to mark. For, following my account of needs in Chapter 1, it would not be enough to say that the primary goods are goods absence of which would create a fundamental harm for the agent. That does not yet capture the full necessity of possession of these goods. Their necessity is a transcendental necessity. The primary goods are goods possession of which is necessary for a person to aspire to active moral agency. A better way of putting this would be to say that they are goods possession of which is a necessary condition for a person to achieve *citizenship*.

The point of pressing a distinction here between goods the distribution of which affects the conditions for citizenship and goods the distribution of which is secondary to it is to note that not all goods should be counted as subject to distribution problems within a market. We must first ensure that the primary goods are available to all to enable and empower individuals into citizenship before we can address the issue of how to settle the distribution problems of secondary goods.

What sorts of goods fall into the primary category? What sorts of goods are those the possession of which is a prerequisite of moral agency and active citizenship? There are no surprises here. The goods in question are possession of access to properly funded education, health and housing that are supplied, managed and regulated according to our best collective notions of the criteria of excellence for each. Education is a key case. The point of counting education provision as an issue concerning the conditions for citizenship is that it takes the supply of education outside the arena of goods over which we engage in distributional debates. It allows us to agree that there is a question of justice concerning the distribution of cars in our society, but not that there is a question of justice concerning the distribution of access to good education. The suggestion is, then, that if members of our society do not have access to education of whatever quality is currently, by the best lights, deemed to constitute excellence, their complaint is not that they suffer an injustice. Their complaint is that they have been denied access to those goods which, in the current development of society, are deemed necessary to achieve full citizenship. Such is the line of argument I wish to deploy.

It will be objected that our notion of the primary goods is constantly in flux. That is true, but it is no objection. It simply marks one dimension of difficulty in putting into practice the requirements of citizenship. The task is not to complete the empowering of individuals into citizenship; it is to ensure that we do not fall into the trap of thinking that goods like educational provision are things to be bargained for, one way or another, in the market for just share-outs. The point is to ensure that we ask the right sorts of questions about the provision of education, health etc., not that we think we can succeed once and for all in getting the provision right.

A further objection will be that the distinction between primary and secondary goods is not as tight as I am supposing. Again, as a practical observation this is correct, but the theoretical import of the distinction is untouched by this remark. The importance of the distinction is perhaps best exemplified if I develop the concept of citizenship that I have appealed to. There are two key models of citizenship, and my claim that justice is not important to the development of socialism is connected with our choice of model. Getting our choice of model right provides us with the argument to count the provision of education, health and housing as constituent parts of the conditions of citizenship and, thereby, removing them from the realm of marketable goods over which we raise distributional problems.

3. Two models of citizenship

We all value the idea of the good citizen, the person who feels a concern for her neighbours and the community around her. But there are two models of citizenship: the individual and social models. In the former the source of the bonds that tie people together arises from the individual. The only condition for citizenship is that individuals have the imaginative resources to reach out to embrace others with their charity. In the latter model, the bonds arise from the community which collectively acts to ensure that certain conditions for citizenship are properly met; here the conditions for citizenship require that society be organised in the appropriate way. On the individual model individuals empower themselves into citizenship. The social model recognises scope for the idea that individuals need to be empowered by the sort of economic and social arrangements in which they find themselves.

On the individual model society does not really exist. We stand alone as isolated individuals and have to construct the bonds of citizenship from resources within and then reach out across a moral vacuum to embrace other individuals. Coming to care for another, coming to see her as a fellow citizen with reciprocal rights, requires a leap of imagination in seeing others like ourselves. The onus lies squarely on the individual to come up with the moral stamina to reach out to others. The distinctive idea behind the social model is that possession of this moral stamina is dependent on the state of the community in which we find ourselves. On the social model, we start as members of a community that predates our individual cares and rights and which supplies us with duties and bonds to others. Although the difference is subtle, it is important.

Consider the workfare idea, the idea that those in receipt of benefits should repay society with an obligation to undertake, say, community work. This is an idea that some on the Left are currently toying with, but it is far from clear that it fits the community model of citizenship.[1] For sure, on the individual model, it seems appropriate to demand that benefit claimants look to find the moral stamina to repay society for its charity. Because the emergence of a reciprocal duty to work in return for the right to benefit depends on nothing but the individual's moral resources, why shouldn't the claimants look to see if they

[1] See Raymond Plant, *Citizens and Rights*, Fabian Society pamphlet (London 1988).

have such resources? And if they haven't, isn't something amiss?

But consider by contrast how the community model of citizenship handles the workfare issue. On this model, citizenship depends on conditions that have to be met collectively, conditions concerning the state of society and the economic and social arrangement of its institutions. For example, it is plausible to think that full and active citizenship requires not just moral courage, but genuine ability to participate in social life. And there is no doubt that those who depend on benefits lack this ability in many ways. Benefit levels do not support genuine options for social engagement from simple matters like being able to buy a daily newspaper to being able to meet one's neighbours socially in the club or pub.[1] And this matters.

After all, if the state gives only a bare subsistence support in benefits why should it expect the citizen to respond with more than subsistence living? If the conditions of active citizenship require that we collectively act to place individuals within a framework that offers genuine options and choices, before we can expect citizenship with its reciprocal duties to the claimant's rights, we have to offer a support that meets the conditions of citizenship. But then, if we are to expect citizenship from claimants, we have to provide a level of benefit far in excess of current levels and, quite probably, in excess of the wages of many who are currently in full employment. And who is prepared to pay that cost of citizenship? Meeting the cost of citizenship would then involve abandoning the presumption that people will only seek work if offered levels of benefit that are frankly degrading. The cost of such citizenship is to give up the free market approach to managing labour supply.[2]

If active citizenship requires the ability to engage in social life there are many dimensions along which this ability can be measured. The most obvious is the one just mentioned, economic ability in the framework of welfare benefit provision.

---

[1] See Beatrix Campbell, *Wigan Pier Revisited* (London 1984), ch. 2, for a graphic account of the extent of life possible on benefit in the UK.

[2] And if a party of the Left decides that it must pledge to run capitalism better than the Tories (as the UK Labour leader promised at the 1988 conference) it is unclear that it could afford this cost.

More fundamental, however, is the way in which our ability to engage in social life is determined by educational and health provisions.

I do not think that there is really anything very contentious in the thought that proper access to good education, health care and housing constitute part of the conditions for citizenship. Take the case of education. The thought is simply this: the proper goal of the education system is the intellectual empowering of people. It is the task of the education system to provide people with the intellectual resources necessary to engage in the complexities of social and economic life as faced in the latter part of the twentieth century. More specifically, the task is one of equipping young people with the analytical skills to assimilate critically and, where necessary, reject information and ideas on offer within our society. What we might call the 'knowledge industry' has a dual role in our society. It is both a central part of human endeavour and an accessory to other areas of human achievement. In the first role, our knowledge industry is no more and no less than our current attempts to fathom the mysteries of the world around us, both the natural and the social world. In this role, it is an integral part of our common culture. But our knowledge industry is also an accessory to other areas of cultural and economic life. In this role it offers people vocational training in preparation for employment. But for young people to be prepared for partnership in both aspects of the knowledge industry they must have access to the highest available standards of education. The vocational side of the educational process is the most obvious from this point of view, but initiation into our common culture is just as much a part of the process of acquiring the habits of mind that make for independence of thought. And without some such habits we cannot attain even a modicum of partnership within the first cultural role of the knowledge industry.

I do not believe anyone will seriously deny the central importance of education in the empowering of people into citizenship, a position within the partnership of our common culture, a position that makes one an active searcher, however humble, after truth. The question is only whether we take the conditions of this citizenship to reside, as in the individual model, within the moral stamina of the individual, or, as in the social model, within structures and institutions provided collectively. And if the argument of the previous chapters is correct we can only opt for the social model of the conditions of citizenship.

For suppose we opted for the individual model of citizenship. What could prompt such a choice? One answer to this question would be acceptance of economism about values. That is, if we thought that there was no such thing as the good and, therefore, no such thing as the criteria of success in provision of education, we would have a good reason for leaving it all to the individual in empowering herself into citizenship. If there are no objective criteria of quality of education provision, then education may as well be treated as a marketable good with individuals free to adopt whatever procedures and types of educational provision they see fit. But of course no one is seriously prepared to admit that there are no objective criteria of quality of education provision. It may be difficult to agree what the criteria are, but if we think that there are such things the only rational option is to try to work them out, not to give up and throw education to the free market. And of course, the whole point of the argument of the previous chapters has been to pursue the claim that there are non-market-oriented goals of success for various arenas of our social life including education.

So without the economism about values that I have argued against it looks as though the only coherent tack is to admit the social model of citizenship. Is this right? Is it possible to preserve the individual model of citizenship but still accept that there are objective criteria that mark out the goals of proper education provision? I do not think that this is a possibility.

The point against the current suggestion is the same as that made in Chapter 4 against withdrawal from the Camelot debate. If there are criteria which pick out the objective goal of education provision, then, however hazy and ill-informed we may be about the exact nature of these criteria, to opt out of the Camelot debate and to attempt to engage these criteria on our own is, in effect, to deny the independent objectivity of the goal we are trying to reach. It is to set oneself up as a master of the good. It is to set oneself up against the authority of the good, and that is a position to which none but the totalitarian can aspire. The only way to ensure that none aspire to, let alone assume such authority is to require that none opt out of the structure of the Camelot debate on education. And that amounts to requiring that education provision should not be treated as a good the distribution of which is to be settled by market criteria of unregulated choice.

If we agree that access to good education is a condition of citizenship and we agree that there are objective criteria that mark out the goal of education provision, we must also accept that the conditions of citizenship are socially determined. The first point, that education is central to proper citizenship, I take as common ground. The second point, that there are objective criteria of the proper goals of education, flows from the central argument of the previous chapters. The conclusion, that the conditions of citizenship are as the social model says, follows from the impossibility of accommodating the objective non-market criteria of good education on the individual model of citizenship.

In practice all this means that education provision should be taken out of the market of tradeable goods; it is a primary good not a secondary one. For the moment, I shall leave this point at this very abstract level. An obvious question to consider is whether there is not still room for issues about the equality or inequality of education provision. For example, suppose the state education sector is deemed to be meeting adequate standards of provision, is it permissible for some schools to opt out of the state sector and to run institutions in the private sector which also, and perhaps better, meet the appropriate standards? In short, doesn't the rather abstract idea about the conditions for citizenship dodge all the difficult questions? I answer this charge in §8. First I want to argue against a popular way of handling questions about the distribution of goods like education.

4. Two theories of justice

Questions about justice are questions about the distribution of goods and services in a society. As already noted, this is not the same as saying that questions about justice are questions about the equality of distribution of goods and services in society. Now many socialists are tempted to deny the approach I have offered and, working within what is essentially an individual model of citizenship, derive arguments against, say, private education from a requirement that the just distribution must be an equal distribution. It is such a line of argument that I now want to defuse.

As I observed in the Introduction, it is useful to distinguish between two different approaches to the theory of justice. I called the approaches the *historical* account of justice and the *end-state* account of justice. On the former, whether or not a distribution of goods and services is just depends on how the distribution came about. On the latter, the justice of a distribution is a matter of the particular end-state pattern of distribution irrespective of how the distribution came into being.

A clear example of an historical theory of justice is that provided by Nozick.[1] Nozick argues for an entitlement theory of justice in which the just distribution of goods is the distribution in which people get what they are entitled to. If we concentrate on property rights entitlements can be understood in the following way.[2] A *basic* entitlement arises when, in a state-of-nature situation, an agent acquires some property from nature by working on it. The only proviso at this point is that in acquiring the property the agent does not infringe the rights of any other agent. A *derived* entitlement is then defined as an entitlement which arises from a free transaction between agents – as, for example, when an agent with a basic entitlement in some property sells it on the free market to another agent. The second agent then has a derived entitlement to the property. If and only if all the holdings in goods and services in a society at a given time t can be traced back to holdings that constitute basic entitlements the distribution of holdings at t is just. In particular, it does not matter if the pattern of holdings at t is, for example, grossly unequal. That is simply irrelevant from the point of view of justice.

It is worth noting at this point that the position I favour employs an entitlement theory of justice. That can seem surprising given the general direction of the argument of this book. But my position is this: I accept an entitlement account

---

[1] R. Nozick, *Anarchy, State and Utopia* (Oxford 1974).

[2] The fact that the theory is best explained in terms of property rights is not insignificant. I return to this in §6 below.

of justice for those goods for which there are problems of distribution. As I have argued that the goods normally thought central to socialist worries about distribution are not to treated as tradeable commodities, this of course is not to accept that entitlement measures of justice are fit for those goods. In other words, because I am arguing that we limit questions of justice, of distribution, to things like cars and continental holidays, there is no difficulty in admitting that the appropriate measure of justice is an entitlement measure. However, before we get to that stage of the argument let me outline an end-state conception of justice.

The key example of an end-state conception of justice is that provided by Rawls.[1] Rawls's position is not so simple to characterise as Nozick's. The reason is that although the theory is clearly designed to provide for a broadly egalitarian constraint on acceptable patterns of distribution, the theory does not directly appeal to equality as a basic value. There is a good reason for the indirectness of Rawls's argument which is worth drawing out before sketching. The reason is that it seems plausible to think of Nozick's entitlement theory of justice as the default option unless some compelling argument can be provided to sustain something stronger. The reason why this is plausible is connected with the predominance of liberalism in our political culture. As noted on many occasions, we are too often tempted to start with the individual who stands alone and for whom we must construct arguments to compel into altruistic concern for others. Given that base, we need an argument why others should be treated as equals worthy of equal concern with ourselves and our immediate family. This starting point is unambiguously endorsed in the opening sentence of Nozick's book:[2]

> Individuals have rights and there are things no person or group may do to them (without violating their rights).

Of course, the whole point of my argument so far has been against this starting point. However, I do accept that if we start here there is no compelling argument to take us any further. Rawls's argument is a good example of many that have

[1] J. Rawls, *A Theory of Justice* (Cambridge, Mass. 1970).
[2] Op. cit., ix.

been constructed in an attempt to take us from the liberal starting point to a more substantive concept of justice than the entitlement theory. Like most commentators, I think the argument fails.[1]

In broad outline Rawls's argument goes like this.[2] The account is a contractualist account. Rawls asks us to consider what sort of contract we would accept for arranging society and its institutions with regard to the distribution of goods in what he calls the 'original position'. The idea of the original position is a device that is meant to lever us from a concern for our own welfare to a concern for the welfare of others. It is the device that is supposed to take us from the liberal starting point to an altruistic notion of justice that has a substantial egalitarian bias. The device works like this. In the original position we conceive of ourselves stripped of knowledge of our social position and intellectual and social equipment. Behind this veil of ignorance we have to strike a contract with our fellows for the arrangement of institutions to distribute goods and services in society. Rawls's suggestion is that the following two principles are pressed as a matter of what it would be rational to agree to under the terms of the original position:[3]

> (1) Each person is to have an equal right to the most extensive basic liberty compatible with a similar liberty for others.

and:

> (2) Social and economic inequalities are to be arranged so that they are both (a) reasonably expected to be to everyone's advantage and (b) attached to positions and offices open to all.

I shall take (1) as a statement of Rawls's underlying liberalism, the presumption he shares with Nozick. The key idea is part (a) of principle (2). This is what Rawls develops as the 'difference principle'. The way that Rawls thinks that inequalities must be to everyone's advantage is that only those inequalities which improve the lot of the worst-off would be acceptable to the rational agent striking contracts in the

---

[1] For a good account of both Nozick's and Rawls's theories of justice, see Alan Brown, *Modern Political Philosophy* (Harmondsworth 1986).

[2] I consider Rawls's later account of his argument in the next section.

[3] Op. cit., 60.

original position. The thought is that *rationality* within the
constraints of the original position requires that agents adopt a
'maximin' strategy; that is, to pursue those courses that ensure
that the worst that can happen to you is as good as possible. The
intuition appealed to here is that in choosing institutions from
behind the veil of ignorance we would have to hedge our bets
against the possibility that, on lifting the veil, we turn out to be
among the worst-off. As that is the worst thing that can happen,
rationality requires that we make that outcome as good as
possible and accept inequalities of distribution only if they
maximise the position of the worst-off.

Rawls's theory has not been short of critics; the flaws are
perhaps obvious. I shall now sketch what the problems are with
a generality that makes it more than probable that the problems
are endemic to any theory which, like Rawls's, tries to derive an
altruistic concern for equality from the liberal starting point.

5. Why Rawls's argument fails

There are two main lines of critique of Rawls's argument. We
can question whether the argument is valid; that is whether
the account is internally coherent. We can also question
whether the argument is compelling; that is, even if it is valid,
do we have any reason to accept its premisses? I shall sketch
each criticism in turn.

The key problem with the validity of the argument lies in the
assumption about what it would be rational to do within the
constraints of the original position. Rawls thinks that the
maximin strategy is a requirement of rationality, but this is
contentious. Consider for a moment the original position and
suppose that, ignorant of your intellectual and social standing,
you are choosing contracts for the distribution of goods and
services within society. Is it really irrational to be prepared to
dispense with the maximin strategy and gamble on an unequal
distribution in the hope that you will turn out to be one of the
favoured well-off? It is simply not apparent what the argument
can be with someone who is prepared to adopt such a strategy.
Of course, quite how much we will be prepared to gamble will
depend on the odds in any given situation. But economic life is
full of people who gamble their life and home for the prospect of
great riches. Whether or not you find yourself able to concur

with such risk-taking, it is simply not convincing to charge such gamblers with irrationality. And that is the charge that Rawls needs to be able to make stick.

Rawls tries to avoid this problem by a number of manoeuvres, but none of them works. For example, he argues that because the choice in the original position is a choice about a 'whole life' the stakes are so high that his cautious maximin strategy is the only rational one. This is simply too weak, as also is his appeal to the value of self-respect and the idea that agents will face loss of self-respect if, in dispensing with the maximin strategy, they end up among the worse-off. Both these points throw up a more substantial worry with Rawls's argument that leads us into the second criticism, that the argument is not compelling. The worry is that both the point about choosing for a 'whole life' and the point about self-respect introduce into Rawls's argument assumptions about what the good life is like to which he is not entitled. If we are to consider the choices in the original position from behind a veil of ignorance, from where do these substantial ideas of the good come? This points to a more serious worry. Even if Rawls were right in his presumption of the maximin strategy as the rational requirement in the original position, why should we share his premisses and find the argument compelling as well as valid?

The point now is that even if the argument was valid, why should it be compelling, for why should the choices that we would make from behind the veil of ignorance have any bearing on what we do and should do from our position of knowledge both of our own situation and that of others? This is a major problem that afflicts all theories which, like Rawls's, attempt to derive substantive moral conclusions from principles of pure rationality alone. One way of expressing the depth of this problem is as follows. The question that Rawls's argument is meant to answer is something like this: 'Why should I endorse distributions which treat others equal to myself?' The argument, if it works at all, works by so dissolving the notion of myself behind the veil of ignorance that differences between myself and others are lost. Then, from the thinness of the ensuing conception, it might look rational to endorse equal distributions. But that is irrelevant to the original question which was why should *I* – the self with current dispositions to treat myself as more important than the selves of others – treat others as equals? The original question, essentially that of how to justify altruism, is ignored by the assumption of the veil of ignorance which effectively blurs the distinctions that make the need for an argument here so pressing.

Another way of putting this point is to ask how I am meant to know what I would choose to contract if I were so radically different from the way that I am to the point of being ignorant of my own intellectual and social standing? Further, what sense can there be to consider *me* divested of knowledge of my desires, intellectual and social standing, etc. After all, if I am divested of all that, surely it is hardly me that I am considering in the original position; it is someone wholly unlike me, as unlike me as it is possible to get. But then, if the argument was an argument to get me to treat *others* as equal, does it not beg the question by making me consider myself so unlike myself as to make the intra-self comparison nothing more than the inter-personal comparison for which, so the original problem has it, there is need of supporting argument? In short, the whole argument scheme looks to derive concern for equal treatment of others only by reducing concern for others to the model of concern for self, in working with a concern for self that is stripped of all that makes me the person I am. And that just short-circuits the whole problem. Concern for others is different from concern for self, that is why there is a problem of justifying anything beyond an entitlement theory once we accept the liberal starting point. That is why I said it is plausible to take Nozick's theory as the default option if no argument away from it can be sustained. Rawls has not offered such an argument.

In later writings Rawls has offered a different account of his position.[1] To see the flaw in the latest version of his argument consider the following summary of the above criticism. Rawls's argument fails because, officially, it is supposed to be an argument with no substantive moral premises. It is designed as an argument which, starting from the liberal position of neutrality, offers considerations of pure rationality which

[1] The central paper is 'Justice as fairness: political not metaphysical', *Philosophy and Public Affairs* (1985).

deliver a substantive moral conclusion in favour of a strongly egalitarian conception of justice. The above two criticisms amount to saying that no such conclusion can be derived from such a thin starting point. The assumption about what it is rational to choose in the original position is not neutral with regard to conceptions of the good life, so the argument is not valid on a thin account of rationality. However, even if the argument were valid, it is not compelling, for the structure of the argument begs the question about the appropriateness of trying to deliver substantive results in such a neutral way. Only someone already committed to egalitarian assumptions will think it appropriate to strip away our notion of ourselves to make us all appear identical and of equal worth, as Rawls does with the device of the original position.

In his paper 'Justice as fairness: political not metaphysical', Rawls denies that his argument has the grand pretensions just attributed to it. In short, he denies that it is supposed to be an argument with no substantive moral premises. By saying that his account of justice is 'political' he means that it is an account of justice fitted to liberal, democratic theory, it is not an account suited to fight off allcomers. The danger now is obvious. By saying this, Rawls stands to lose all normativity of his position and his theory amounts to no more that a complicated, albeit elegant, description of the sort of account of justice most liberals would endorse. Well, that might be so. But unless and until he can give some independent argument why, for example, Nozick is not a liberal, the theory is no more than a grand intellectual construction that can offer no leverage against the default option of Nozick's entitlement theory.

6. Why Nozick's argument fails

I have spent some time outlining the argument against Rawls's account of justice. I have done this because many think that it, or something like it, provides a foundation for an egalitarian system of distribution. The counter-arguments that I have sketched are widely accepted, but in accepting them in the context of this book it might be thought that I have dangerously given away too much to what I have called the default option. I do not think that this is the case. The reason is clear: Nozick's account, although internally, I think, much stronger than Rawls's, suffers dramatically from the lack of any argument in support of his starting point – the basic liberalism and economism of values.

Now, in one sense, the lack of argument for Nozick's starting point does not matter. What Nozick offers is a crisp and cleverly articulated account of what follows if you start out from the individualism of liberalism, from the image of individuals alone with only their rights for protection. However, rather than accept the ensuing entitlement theory of justice, I take Nozick's case as a *reductio ad absurdum* of the starting point. I am prepared to agree with Nozick that, given his starting point, inequality of distribution of goods and services is not an injustice, but as I have argued at length against that starting point I do not have to accept the conclusion. In which case I do not need to tackle Nozick's argument in detail, for I have already argued for a richer starting point in our political deliberations than Nozick's.

7. A plague on both their theories

Although I do not have to accept Nozick's conclusion that inequality of distribution of goods is not an injustice, nevertheless I do accept it. However, this is possible only because I have argued that the things the distribution of which socialists typically worry about are not 'goods' in the sense of items to be distributed by the principles of entitlement or, for that matter, by any other principles. The items in question are preconditions for citizenship that must be firmly in place for all citizens before we can raise distribution questions about secondary goods. In saying this, I am arguing against the theories of both Rawls and Nozick.

In particular I am arguing against their common assumption, the assumption of a liberal neutrality about the good. My argument has been of a kind with the argument begun in Chapter 1 about the centrality of the concept of the good for a viable political philosophy. In the light of the argument of Chapter 3, there is an alternative argument available against the core presupposition of both the theories of justice considered here. The argument turns on a charge of the ideological character of that presupposition. I shall sketch the argument here.

Let us consider Nozick's position, for that is the clearer case. The key assumption is the inviolability of the individual and her rights. Having acquired a holding in goods and services which, in acquisition, violates no one else's rights, the individual agent is entitled to do with her holding just as she sees fit. She may give it away, sell it, exchange it at whatever price she is happy to accept and so on. It is worth considering the following question: What sorts of holdings look to be the central concerns of the patterns of entitlement that Nozick outlines? I think the answer is clear. The holdings for which the theory of entitlement looks to be specifically designed to defend are property holdings: more generally, holdings in capital and other commodities. Following a long line of theorists Nozick seems to be assuming that the primary business of a theory of justice is to preserve and safeguard people's property rights and capital rights.

The entitlement theory captures the logic of the market in capital and other commodities with precision. Holdings in capital are just if and only if they are such that they came about in a certain sort of way. And the way that the entitlement theory takes as appropriate is just the way that leaves the market wholly unregulated with regard to, for example, desirable end-states. All that matters with regard to Nozick's theory is that the market in holdings should operate freely.

It is no accident that the account of just holdings entailed by Nozick's theory delivers just the right account for a free-market capitalist economy in which all goods are to be freed from end-state accounts of a good distribution. But the problem this raises is now this. Nozick's key assumption is constitutive of his theory. If we buy that assumption we will be persuaded by the arguments Nozick offers in favour of the entitlement theory, but what reason is there to buy that assumption? Now I argued, in Chapter 1, that the underlying individualism at issue here was untenable. The argument had its roots in abstract matters about the nature of moral rules and the impossibility of capturing the normativity of moral values on the individualist conception. If, in the light of those arguments, we can see no argument in support of Nozick's starting point, can we not now support a challenge of ideology along the lines suggested in Chapter 3? First, we note that the reasoning in support of the theory is implicitly circular in that its validity depends on the key individualistic assumption which is constitutive of the theory. We then charge that the circularity of reasoning involved from within the individualist conception, given lack of independent argument for the key assumption, threatens to take the theory out of the realm of cognition. The disjunctive challenge from the theory of ideology is then this: Either the individualist gives some independent non-circular defence of the key assumption, or we conclude that the theory is held not as a rational belief supportable with good reasons, but as an ideological belief because (causal) it supports the underlying capitalist free-market in capital and commodities.

I do not want to do any more than sketch a line of argument here. There are a number of points that need much elaboration and defence for the charge of ideology to stick. For the moment I merely want to indicate the possibility of such a line of argument. For example, the idea that a functional explanation may be forthcoming for why a Nozickian theory seems compelling in virtue of its support for a capitalist free-market needs much support. It is not enough just to notice that a function of the entitlement theory is to support such a market economy. That, I assume is pretty uncontentious. Capital, if it is to achieve maximum profit ratios, needs the unrestricted freedom to be exchanged, transferred and deployed wherever profits can be made typical of the sort of account of just holdings and exchanges delivered by the entitlement theory. But that does not show that there is a functional explanation why that theory has such a grip on the minds of modern political theorists. It simply points us in the direction of seeing if such an explanation is available.

Similarly, we need also to show that there is an explanatory puzzlement why so many should adopt such a starting point in political theorising. That is probably a much harder task given the enormous consensus that such individualism is the right starting point.

I shall not discharge these requirements here. To do so would involve too long a detour from my main line of argument, and it is not clear to me, at this point, what the best way of conducting such a detour would be. I mention the possibility of putting together some such charge of the ideological character of the starting point common to both

Nozick and Rawls only to draw out a point that has been bobbing beneath the surface of my argument for some time now. The point is that on my conception of the proper way of going about moral and political argument there is no clear demarcation between our factual social scientific investigations of society and our evaluative accounts of society. Too often moral and political theory assumes that there is a clear demarcation here. Furthermore, it expects moral theory to come up with a rigorous decision procedure for handling problem cases which will, once and for all, give a resolution to dilemmas that can be shown to be rationally incontrovertible. This model of moral and political theorising owes much to the predominance of utilitarian thought in our culture. I think this model is fundamentally mistaken. The most, it seems to me, that moral and political theory can offer is some guidelines about the presuppositions of our moral and political thought and some sketch of the proper way of conducting such thought. When it comes to particular cases, there is no getting away from the fact that our moral lives are messy complicated affairs and that any philosopher who offers a general decision procedure as a panacea for our ills is either a fraud or a utilitarian.[1]

8. Some difficult questions

I must now return to the charge I raised at the end of §3. The charge was that in arguing for the provision of education, health and housing as conditions of citizenship I had dodged all the difficult questions. The difficult questions are questions like, 'What level of health care is a condition of citizenship?', 'What kind of access to education is a condition of citizenship?' etc. And then, so the charge might continue, in handling these questions we will have to employ the concept of equality despite the argument of the last four sections. I do not think this charge sticks.

First, these questions are not really my concern. My concern is, as ever, with the legitimacy of interference in education provision. If we are to act so as to regulate education provision

[1] The influence of Bernard Williams's conception of moral theory will be evident here to any who know his *Ethics and the Limits of Philosophy* (London 1986).

and not leave it a good to be put on the free market and sold to the highest bidders, we have to be sure that we are able to ask the right questions. The above questions are the right questions. My concern in this book is to ensure that it is such questions that we ask, not directly to sketch the answers. If my argument prompts such questions, all well and good, it is meant to! The point is that these are the sorts of questions the answers to which should guide the way we regulate education provision, rather than questions such as, 'Is the distribution of education provision just or fair?' For if that were our question then, lacking a cogent argument against the entitlement theory, we lack any legitimate complaint against an education system in which most of the resources are directed at a few. If the only objection against that is to say it is unequal, why is that a complaint? My argument has been to suggest that the complaint, if there is one, should arise from the way we answer the question 'What level of education provision is a condition for citizenship?' If a system does not provide an education system for sections of the community that meets the conditions for citizenship, its failing is not the abstract notion of the inequity of distribution, but its denial of citizenship to portions of the community.

I do not pretend to have the answers to all the particular issues that arise when we start asking questions like 'What level of education provision is a condition for citizenship?' and I am not a utilitarian. My concern is to provide the conceptual resources that make the demand to regulate central areas of our society, like education and health, a legitimate demand. My concern is to map the conceptual repertoire that justifies the interference in the supply of these things which, from the perspective of the liberal, cannot be justified. On the liberal individualistic conception, these things must be counted as tradeable goods, for without the authority of the good the liberal has no legitimate complaint against those who wish to employ their wealth to corner the supply in health care and education. The liberal will complain that this is not *fair*, but without a cogent argument against the entitlement theory this complaint gives no legitimacy to intervention.

Our predominant culture is an entitlement culture in which we normally start our political debates from the individualistic starting point of the liberal. My concern is to articulate the alternative conceptual map which alone can legitimate the sorts of concerns and interferences that have been typical of socialists. I have also argued that the alternative conceptual map, centred on the authority of the good and now employing a social model of citizenship, is the only viable conceptual map, for without the Good Principle the notion of the good collapses altogether. If these theoretical arguments about the general structure of the agenda for socialism are right, that is enough for now. My conception of political theory does not permit me or encourage me to think that I can derive determinate decision procedures so that, as well as settling the theoretical outline of socialism, I go on to provide detailed policy initiatives. That is not a philosophical enterprise. It is an enterprise that will involve many disciplines and contributors. It is no more and no less than an exercise in the Camelot debate.

I think the above answers the main part of the charge that I posed. However, the charge contained also this thought: In handling the questions about the levels of education, health care, etc. that are conditions for citizenship will it not be the case that the concept of equality will still play a large part? Alternatively, am I committed to the idea that, beyond some specified level of provision which constitutes the conditions of citizenship, education, health etc. can be traded on the market and inequities in provision arise? These questions are legitimate theoretical questions that need to be answered.

9. Equality does not matter

Take the situation of education provision as it exists in the UK today. Suppose we identify the level of provision found in the state education sector, call it L. Outside the state sector education provision is also found in the private sector. Suppose that is a level of $L+n$. Now, if level L were found to constitute a level adequate to meet the conditions of citizenship, my argument could then offer no complaint that those with the necessary resources can purchase a higher level of provision than the majority. For, to make that complaint, surely we would need to invoke the concept of equality, the role of which as a fundamental premiss I am denying. At best, the only complaint possible would depend on the shaky empirical argument about what constitutes an adequate level of education provision to meet the conditions for citizenship.

This challenge has to be met in two respects. First, there is a question whether we *should* complain at a situation like the one outlined. Secondly, there is the question whether my argument gives ground for complaint. Given the direction my argument has taken I cannot answer the first question until I have answered the second. Of course, we may feel upset at inequities as postulated, but, on the presumption of the correctness of my argument so far, whether there is a legitimate complaint will turn solely on whether my argument gives ground for complaint. That is, I accept that, if my argument gives no ground for complaint, we should not complain at the situation. However, I think my argument does give ground for complaint.

The reason why my argument does not support the envisaged situation is due to the *open-endedness* of the concept of citizenship. The situation envisaged poses a problem only if we make two assumptions. The first is that the conditions of citizenship can be fixed at a certain level of education provision. The second is the empirical assumption that level L constitutes the fixed level. My response to the situation does not rely on challenging the second assumption. Rather I deny the first.

By saying that the concept of citizenship is open-ended I mean that there are no fixed levels of education and health provision that constitute achievement of citizenship. There is no point at which we can say that so-and-so has now achieved citizenship and the rest is surplus. My reason for saying this is not that I want to fix the conditions of citizenship at some ideal level. It is rather that I want to deny that the conditions can be fixed at determinate levels at all. This is a claim about the nature of the concept of citizenship. I want to defend this claim with an analogy.

Take the idea that the role of the education service is to enable individuals to realise their full potential in various skills both intellectual and social. Now the idea of achieving your potential is an idea of something which has no fixed level. It would be senseless to stop educating a child, to think she had realised her ideal, just because she had achieved some predetermined goal set down by educationalists. The idea of a person's intellectual potential is open-ended. In the same way the concept of citizenship is an open-ended idea. Because our society is continually evolving and issuing new challenges to its members it is not possible to lay down in advance the exact level that a person has to achieve in order to achieve citizenship. Just as our knowledge industry is ever growing and it is not possible to lay down an exact upper level, attainment of which would constitute reaching one's intellectual potential, so it is not possible to do the same with the upper level for citizenship. There is no level beyond which provision is a luxury.

The general point here is this. Our idea of the intellectual potential of an individual varies with our ideas about the size and complexity of our knowledge industry. Achievements which would once have seemed, relative to their time, achievements over which there could be no upper level, now seem relatively modest. If we fix levels of potential achievement we stunt our collective advance in the knowledge industry. But similarly, our notion of citizenship varies with our ideas about the size, complexity and organisation of society. Standards of citizenship which would have done well in city-state communities – for example, an ability at oratory – are not necessarily adequate conditions for active participation in modern society. If we fix upper levels of the conditions of citizenship and thereby treat provision above that as luxuries, we stunt our collective advance in the development of our civil polities.

Now the effect of this is to demand that there should be no inequities in provision of those things like education, health and housing that we count as conditions of citizenship. For if we accept the open-endedness of the concept of citizenship we cannot concede that there is any point at which it is legitimate to allow the provision of education to be put on the commodity market. Once that is done and access to education, access to the conditions of citizenship, is made a function of ability to pay we have sown the seeds for different classes of citizenship. The conditions of citizenship do not require access to a particular level of education and health care, after which all else is surplus; rather, the conditions of citizenship require access to an open-ended provision of education, health care, etc. And the only way to ensure that the provision is open-ended is to ensure that these goods are not offered on the free market. The conclusion comes not from an abstract demand for equality which, in face of the default option of the entitlement theory cannot be justified. The conclusion comes from an account of the concept of citizenship. If you want to put the conclusion in terms of equality, it must be realised that this is a derived demand for equality. What is important is the source from which that demand issues.

10. Paying for citizenship

Suppose the above arguments are right. Who is to pay for the provision of the primary goods which are required in order to meet the conditions of citizenship? The obvious answer is that we all pay through a system of progressive taxation. But why is this answer obvious? For sure, it can seem obvious to all concerned that, if education, health care and some provision for housing are primary goods then they should be provided for out of the state's tax revenues, but is this legitimate and why should the taxation system be a progressive one?

On the first point. If the whole point of primary goods is that they must be taken out of the market of tradeable commodities, there is no option but to fund them out of general taxation. But taxation is itself an area in which liberals can feel uneasy about the legitimacy of distribution. However, once again the problems arise from asking the wrong question. If we ask if the taxation system is *just*, what justification is there, short of a cogent argument against the default option of the entitlement theory, in taking money from individuals to provide a benefit for all? On the default option, surely the right method would be to leave every person to provide, if she so wishes, education for her children to the standard she wishes. But this simply flies in the face of the whole of my argument to date. On the position that I have been outlining this is simply not an option. Let us just be clear why.

Our concern with the conditions of citizenship is a concern for the health of society, not with the health of individuals. There is a social dimension to the good; there is a good about the way our society is as well as the good about the way individual lives are. It is in meeting the requirement that we achieve a good society, a civil polity, that we need to meet the conditions of citizenship. And that is why the responsibility for this provision falls on us all collectively. That being so, the provision must be funded from collective resources, taxation. The denial of this that I have just canvassed depends on a wholesale commitment to individualism and economism about values that I have been attacking thoughout this book. Meeting the conditions of citizenship is undertaken in order to make our society, a collection of citizens, possible. It is not done to enable success for individuals, but to enable success for citizens: people with a moral and social role within a larger framework, a civil polity. Meeting the conditions of citizenship is then *our* responsibility; it falls on us all. General taxation to meet the provision of primary goods is then legitimate. It is challenged only by breaking with the conceptual scheme that I have been putting together throughout the argument of this book.

But is there any reason why the taxation system should be a progressive one that takes more taxes from those with higher incomes? If we start with an abstract demand for equality a progressive taxation system is then justified as a component of the drive to achieve equality. But I have broken with that starting point. What I want to suggest is this. Once more, given that meeting the conditions of citizenship is a responsibility that falls on us all, not only is taxation the right source of funding, but also, other things being equal, it is legitimate to take more taxes from those more able to pay. However, I want to qualify this by noting that it gives no licence for continually progressive tax rates. That is, if at any time society finds its resources for primary goods adequate, there is no justification for further higher rates of taxation upon those with large incomes. Such attempts to use the taxation system as a general tool of levelling is not legitimate, for it depends only on the spurious abstract demand for equality (or perhaps pure spite) and that is not justified.

So, on the question of the progressive nature of taxation there are two points to be made. First, given a need for the health of our society, education provision of a generally agreed level must be funded. Only then will our society continue to evolve with its members achieving active citizenship. Now this provision could not be funded by simply taking an equal share from all those in employment, for if the share is to be affordable to those of low incomes it would not suffice. However, that fact does not justify the idea of a meagre provision of whatever level could be supported with an equal share deduction, with the rest left to the private market, for that reneges on the argument of the last section. It is our responsibility to see that our society flourishes. This is a collective responsibility. And if adequate funding by equal deduction only served to disable some contributors in other areas of social life, we cannot demand of those on low incomes that they give more than can be afforded. But we are not so constrained with those on higher incomes. It can look like this only if we succumb to the liberal model of isolated individuals, each looking to strike a profitable bargain in the market. But that is not how things are. We are concerned to provide for the health of our society, and it is the social collective nature of the need that legitimates the idea that those who can afford more should pay more. This is not a contract for them to ponder and calculate; it is a legitimate demand placed upon them as members of a society that is trying to ensure its future health and the conditions of citizenship for its next generation.

The second point that needs to be made is this. Because the demand for progressive taxation does not depend on the abstract demand for equality, the notion of progressive taxation is not extendable beyond the point at which we have met the currently agreed conditions of citizenship. That is, it is not an abstract demand that the higher the income the higher the tax. Just suppose that no one earns more than 60,000 and we fix tax rates such as the following:

<15,000	25%
15,001 – 25,000	30%
25,001 – 40,000	40%
40,001 – 60,000	50%

The exact figures do not matter. The point I want to make is this. If in fixing these rates there were no people who earned in excess of 60,000 there is no legitimate reason why, once such earners appear, they should be expected to pay a further higher rate of tax. It is not automatic that tax rates should carry on increasing with levels of income. It depends only on whether there are still matters of primary goods provision to be settled and whether that requires more revenue than currently available. And if there is no such requirement, there is no legitimacy for further higher bands of taxation. The abstract distributional point that those on very high levels of income are not, in such cases, paying taxes in the same proportion of earned income as those lower down the scale has no bite on the account that I am providing. In short, if you are able to earn a high income that fact alone does not license a government to take a higher proportion of it away from you in taxes than it takes from those not able to earn so much. The need for progressive taxation is not a distributional need; it is not undertaken to redistribute wealth. Progressive taxation is undertaken to meet the conditions of citizenship for all members of society. Once again, this may well have the effect of licensing familiar sorts of progressive taxation systems, but the legitimacy has a different source to the one usually offered. The demand for equality offers no legitimacy, the demand to meet the conditions of citizenship does.

6

Democracy and the Rule of Law

Democracy is concerned with the empowerment of people. However, depending on our understanding of the concept of empowerment, we get from this slogan different accounts of democracy. In this chapter I shall give a brief sketch of the account of democracy that flows from the argument of the preceding chapters. In doing this I shall also touch on the difficult question of whether the rule of law is sacrosanct.

1. Democracy and empowerment

The concept of democracy is a slippery notion. The simple answer to the question 'What is a democracy?' is that it is a polity governed by the people, the *demos*. But the usual follow-up question, 'What institutional arrangements need to be in place for government to be by the people?', invites such an array of replies that we are soon led to conclude that

> Democratic theory is the moral Esperanto of the present nation-state system, the language in which all Nations are truly United, the public cant of the modern world, a dubious currency ... and one which only a complete imbecile would be likely to take at face value.[1]

Nevertheless I think it is possible to extract an element of the idea of empowering people that captures an important core to the concept of democracy.

It is customary in discussions of democracy to distinguish between ancient and modern versions of the idea.

[1] J. Dunn, *Western Political Theory in the Face of the Future* (Cambridge 1979), 2.

157

Schumpeter's celebrated distinction between classical democracy and what he called his 'modern alternative' is a case in point. He defined classical democracy as follows:[1]

> The democratic method is that institutional arrangement for arriving at political decisions which realises the common good by making the people itself decide issues through the election of individuals who are to assemble in order to carry out its will.

Scepticism about the cogency of the ideas of the common good and the common will led him to offer a modern alternative definition:[2]

> The democratic method is that institutional arrangment for arriving at political decisions in which individuals acquire the power to decide by means of a competitive struggle for the people's vote.

In Schumpeter's terms the distinction between the two turns on the availability of something called the common good and the will of the people. I think we can get a clearer picture of the underlying conceptual issues with the notion of democracy if we start with a tripartite distinction, for Schumpeter's distinction does not make clear an issue that I want to draw out. The issue is concerned with the sorts of empowerment various institutional arrangements are designed to effect.

So, let us return to the opening thought that a democracy is a polity governed by the people. Before rushing on with the question 'What institutional arrangements need to be in place for government to be by the people?' let us first consider the simplest possible model of democracy.

In the simple model we need to consider a social grouping which is small enough in population and geographical distribution to enable direct participation by all its members. In the terminology of Chapter 4, we consider a grouping in which all *bona fide* members can participate in the Camelot debate. In the simple model we are considering a small community in which face-to-face encounters suffice to provide methods for co-ordinating decisions of the group. Such a group

---

[1] J.A. Schumpeter, *Capitalism, Socialism and Democracy* (2nd ed., London 1942), 250.
[2] Ibid., 269.

is democratic if all its members have the power to participate in decision making by the simple act of engaging in discourse with their fellows. Such small face-to-face groups are often thought of as the ideal model of a democracy. Call such a case the direct Camelot model of democracy. In this model there is direct participation by all *bona fide* members of the group. We should note two features of such a simple case.

First, implicit in my reference to *'bona fide* members of the group' is the point that such a model provides us with a further facet of the concept of citizenship. Depending on what we mean by 'power' we might say that citizens are those with the power to participate in collective decision-making. Of course, this leaves it open that there may be people who, although members of the group, do not possess citizenship because they are, for various reasons, excluded from participation. The reasons for exclusion may be plausible or not; for example, exclusion may be for reasons of youth, senility, race or sex. If there is an excluded category of members of the group, they are not empowered by the method of decision-making used by the group and are not thereby citizens of the group. And of course it seems obvious that there must always be some exclusion group. The issues touched on here are really concerned with the legitimacy of the many exclusion principles that have been employed through human history.

Secondly, in the direct Camelot model, there is no issue about the institutional arrangements that need to be in place for government to be by the people. The arrangements are simply the arrangements of normal social and linguistic intercourse. In the direct Camelot model the conclusion of a debate generally ends not with a vote but with the realisation, 'Well, that's agreed then.' Perhaps there are few instances left in contemporary society of the direct Camelot model, but the possibility of such a model is clear. So, in the direct Camelot model there is no further question about the institutional arrangements that need to be in place to enable decision-making to occur. Decision making flows from the patterns of normal social intercourse. It flows from the common sharing of places within a Camelot debate. In other words, in the direct Camelot model the very size of the community ensures that there is such a thing as the common good and the will of the people. Of course, this is not to deny that in reaching a decision some citizens will have to give way and amend their beliefs and plans. But in the direct Camelot model such giving way does not consist in forming an opposition party or organisation which then tries at a later stage to reverse the decision. In the direct Camelot model giving way is an act of acceptance. The community simply is not big enough to accommodate non-acceptance. It is one of the advantages of life in a small community that one is forced to live with others whose views one may not share. One has no option but to find ways of agreeing and living together. The option of ignoring those with whom one does not agree, or even plotting to thwart their plans is simply not available, for there are insufficient numbers to make such actions effective. Living in large urban communities, we treat as natural the ability to chose our friends and associates with some care to ensure that we mix only with those for whom we feel an affinity. Pleasing and reassuring though this may be, it is a luxury and something that blinds us to the mechanisms of agreement and living that occur in the direct Camelot model of democracy.

Now, of course, the direct Camelot model is a utopian ideal. It is only applicable in small commune-type societies, but getting it in focus enables us to mark more accurately the difference between Schumpeter's classical and modern accounts of democracy.

Let us then consider the second model of democracy. This is the ancient model exemplified in the institutions arranged by the Athenians of classical times. I shall call this 'the indirect Camelot model' in order to note a common feature with the simple Camelot model. The indirect Camelot model comes about when we consider a community too large and diverse for the direct Camelot model to apply. However, what is important about this second model is that the institutional arrangements it employs are not merely arrangements for arriving at a decision; they are arrangements for arriving at a decision validated by a Camelot debate. In the second model it may not be possible to get everyone into the debating chamber, but it is at least possible to get representatives of the people into the chamber and then expect them to conclude their deliberations just as the community does in the direct Camelot model. In other words, this second model is the same as Schumpeter's account of classical democracy, for the institutional arrangements that it employs are required to ensure that a representative sample of the community deliberate to work out the common good.

Contrast this with the third model. Following a suggestion of Dahl's, I shall call this the polyarchical model of democracy.[1] The definitive point about the polyarchical model is that the institutional arrangments of a democracy are arrangements designed primarily to give power to various individuals or groups to form, for a limited time, a dictatorship. It is the fact that the dictatorship is only held for a limited time which makes this a polyarchical arrangement or, as Dahl puts its, a 'government by minorities' not a government by minority.[2]

There is then a contrast between the first and second models, which have something in common, and the third model. It is not easy to be precise what it is that the first two models have in common. We may put it that they both assume the availability of a notion of the common good, but that is rather hazy. Although it is certainly the case that the third model denies this notion, effectively reducing the business of democracy to sorting out the various power-play relationships between groups in society. Further, there is little doubt that it is the third model which most closely fits the democratic process at the national level in those countries that call themselves democracies.[3] For example, consider the following definition of democracy given by a leading contemporary theorist. Democracy is characterised[4]

> by a set of rules ... which establish *who* is authorised to take collective decisions and which *procedures* are to be applied.

And note that the issues centre on the question of how to select those who are to be granted power to decide, rather than the sort of decisions, for example, for the common good, that they

---

[1] R. Dahl, *A Preface to Democratic Theory* (Chicago 1956).

[2] Ibid., 133.

[3] Note that I make this as a descriptive point, not a normative point about the legitimacy of this model of democracy. There are clear problems with Dahl's idea of government by minorities, most obviously with his assumption that minorities' influence on governments will vary proportionately with intensity of political feeling expressed in terms of intensity of political activity on the part of pressure groups. This is a highly contentious empirical assumption. For a clear discussion of this and related issues see J. Lively, *Democracy* (Oxford 1975), 20ff.

[4] Norberto Bobbio, *The Future of Democracy*, ed. R. Bellamy, trans. R. Griffin (Cambridge 1987) 24.

are to strive for. However, in order to be precise about what it is that separates these models, we must turn to examine the notion of empowerment and the different forms it takes under the first and second as contrasted with the third model of democracry.

2. Two models of empowerment: the economic and the moral

If we say that democracy is about the empowerment of people, what do we mean by empowerment? The simple answer is this: democracy obtains when the members of a community are granted political power in the decision-making processes of the community. That sounds a rather glib answer. It looks a little less glib if rephrased as 'Democracy requires that citizens achieve political agency'. Now, I take it that it is *that* which constitutes the eternal appeal of the utopian ideal of the direct Camelot model of democracy. Democrats everywhere endorse the rightness of that model, and only bemoan its inapplicability in a modern industrial society. The question now is whether or not the feature which constitutes the core to the appeal of the direct Camelot debate is detachable from the romantic idealism of commune life. I think that it is.

The idea that democracy requires that citizens achieve political agency, indeed that if they do not achieve political agency they do not achieve citizenship, gives us a marker for distinguishing the first and second models of democracy from the third. I shall call the first and second models of democracy models that provide a *thick* conception of democracy as opposed to the *thin* conception achieved on the third model. The reason for this distinction is that on a thick conception of democracy the community's decisions are decisions that are made under the conditions of a Camelot debate. That is, they are decisions that are made in a debate that defers to the authority of the good. The point is that in either of the first two models a decision is justified just in case the participants to the debate have arrived at that decision in a way that acknowledges the various criteria of good relevant to the decision at hand. Of course, in either of the first two models the participants may get it wrong. They may make mistakes in applying the relevant criteria or in mistaking what the appropriate criteria are. That does not matter. What does matter is that the decision-making process is responsive to debate about the appropriate criteria of good. That is the point of the idea of deferring to the authority of the good. And in these models the participants to the debate, in entering a debate that defers to the authority of the good, engage in full political agency. On the second, indirect Camelot model, not all citizens can participate thus, but if the institutional arrangements for selecting the participants are, as in the classical Athenian model, arranged so as to support multifaceted relations of accountability between officials and citizens, then all citizens are close enough to the debate to make it plausible to say that all are activating their political agency.[1]

However, in the third model of democracy, the polyarchical model, a decision is justified simply in virtue of its having been endorsed by those who find themselves with the majority power to force the decision through. There is no requirement that the decision defer to whatever criteria of assessment may be thought applicable. Once elected, a government can pursue whatever policies it wishes. And although it must always have an eye on its popularity when the next election comes around, experience shows that the next election is often a long way off and all manner of devices can be employed to ensure a happy profile when it comes. However a government employs its effective dictatorship, the point remains that it is not part of the institutional arrangements of a polyarchical democracry that its decisions are validated by how well they stand up to the authority of the good. And that is why I call it a thin conception of democracy, in contrast to both the direct and the indirect Camelot models.

The contrast turns on the question of what validates a collective decision. On the thick conception of democracy the institutional arrangements, if any, that need to be in place to secure a democratic polity are such that the validity of a collective decision derives from the way these arrangements enshrine deference to the authority of the good. The arrangements are designed to enforce a Camelot style debate in decision-making in which the decision is ratified in terms of

---

[1] For details of the institutional arrangement of Athenian democracy see David Held, *Models of Democracy* (Oxford & Cambridge 1987), ch. 1.

the appropriate non-market criteria of good. On the thin conception of democracy, the validity of a collective decision turns on no more than that the institutional arrangements ensure that no one group can guarantee its continued dominance in policy-making. In other words, the thin conception of democracy enshrines the disappearance of the good criticised in Chapter 1.

Another way of marking this distinction is by answering the following question: If a democracy empowers people to give them a role in the decision-making processes of a community, what is the empowering relation? More specifically, if empowered citizens are those with the power to effect the decisions in a polity, what is this relation of effect? It is this question that we can answer by distinguishing two models of empowerment which capture the difference between thick and thin conceptions of democracy. Now clearly, in all but the direct Camelot model of democracy citizens do not have the opportunity to exercise their political agency; they must elect representatives to act on their behalf. However, we can mark the two models of empowerment if we look at the empowerment relation in terms of the sort of accountability representatives bear to the citizens.

I want to distinguish between what I call economic empowerment and moral empowerment. The former provides only for a thin notion of democracy, the latter for a thick notion. What differentiates these two kinds of empowerment is the sort of accountability relation representatives bear to citizens. In economic empowerment, the representatives are accountable to the citizens simply in virtue of the fact that their right to continue in the role as representative must, from time to time, be renewed in an election. In moral empowerment, the representatives are accountable to the citizens not only in having their power endorsed from time to time at elections, but for their observance or non-observance of the terms of the Camelot debates about the good which determine collective decisions. Under economic empowerment representatives, once elected, are free to make decisions by whatever criteria they deem fit with no further deference to the electorate or the authority of the good. There is no sense of a stronger bond between electorate and elected than the need to win another licence to govern at a future election. I call this 'economic

empowerment' because the accountability relation is so thin
and signals no real common purpose between electorate and
representative. They meet only every four or five years, and
when they meet they are bound by no norms other than the
representatives' desire to be re-elected and the electorate's
desire to get value for their vote. As such, the relation is like
that of consumer and vendor in a commodity market.[1] This is
not the case with moral empowerment.

Now moral empowerment is a difficult notion. What I mean
to signal is a situation where the empowerment relation
between representative and electorate, the relation of
accountability, is such that there are more things that tie the
two together than the simple market model of economic
empowerment. Clearly, under the direct Camelot model all
citizens are also representatives, for all participate in the
debates about common policy and they are bound together by
no less than the moral norms that define their shared living
and attempts to achieve a common notion of the good life. But
once we move to consider the indirect Camelot model under
which we have a distinction between electorate and
representatives, it is tempting to think that problems of scale
necessitate a slide into the third model of polyarchical
democracy. That is, it is tempting to think that problems of
scale demolish the scope for the second model. I think this is
wrong, but if we are to substantiate the second model, if
something more than economic empowerment is to be possible
once we have a distinction between the electorate and the
representatives, then we cannot simply leave the need for
greater bonds between the two to the pious wish for greater
deference to the authority of the good. We must actually do
something to ensure that more than economic empowerment
becomes the norm. The obvious way to act here is as follows.

For the indirect Camelot model of democracy to be possible
we must set up structures that closely define and constrain the
accountability relation between citizens and their representatives. We cannot leave it that, once elected, representatives
can behave in whatever way they wish, constrained only by the
need to win enough vote capital at the next election to be

[1] See I. McLean, *Public Choice* (Oxford 1987), ch. 3 for the use of this analogy
in an analysis of voter behaviour.

re-elected. That is not good enough. We need to constrain the accountability relation more tightly and define the legitimate domains of decision and excutive action. In short, for the indirect Camelot model of democracy to be so much as possible, we need extensive legislation to set the framework for our democratic practices.

Under the terms of the limited size of Athenian democracy institutional arrangements were legislated for that guaranteed that officials did not enjoy the sort of freedom that representatives enjoy under modern democracy in the UK. But the arrangements that the Athenians employed are ill-suited to polities of modern size. For example, in Athens office was filled by lot, and for as many as possible it was held for as short a time as possible. Thus the streamlined committe of 50 which led the Council of 500 which, in turn, was responsible for the agenda and organisation of the Assembly (quorum 6,000) was led by a President whose office lasted for one day only. On top of that, many offices were restricted so that a citizen could hold it only once. Requirements such as these could not work in a large industrial society. But there are requirements that can be imposed that would help to create a richer relation of accountability between representatives and the electorate. The requirements are that there should be a body of *constitutional law* which defines and structures the democratic process and the relations and arrangements which legitimise it.

Obvious instances of such requirements are: a Bill of Rights to define and sustain central civil liberties like the right to peaceful assembly, trial by jury, freedom of expression; a Freedom of Information Bill without which any more extensive accountability relation than that of economic empowerment would be a farce; a constitutionally defined separation of the legislative and executive powers, but with the latter firmly under the control of parliament with all state agencies subject to the rule of law; reform of the House of Lords to establish an elected second chamber; and, most important of all, a clear constitutional demarcation of the distribution of power between local, regional and national government.

There is nothing new in these requirements.[1] My point is

---

[1] As recently as December 1988, the need for a detailed written constitution has been promoted in a document called Charter 88 drawn up by a non-party collection of academics, arts and media personnel as well as politicians. See

only this. The requirement that we settle a written constitution governing the accountability relation between government and governed is a requirement that flows from the need to develop the scope for a model of democracy in which citizens are empowered in the full sense of achieving political agency. I have stressed throughout this book the necessity for a socialist government to pursue policies which dethrone the needs of capital and market criteria of success and replace them with attempts to fashion the non-market criteria of success that come from regaining the authority of the good. So, in the area of education, health and housing a socialist government must *start* its policy formulation from a considered account of the appropriate non-market criteria of success in these domains. The starting point for a socialist administration must be a clear formulation of the sort of society it wants to bring about. But there is another side to this business of articulating a vision of the good life; there is the matter of arranging the democratic institutions of our society so as to encourage the renewed deference to the good.

A socialist administration can chain Capital and attempt to set people free from the bonds of the market, but unless it also provides the institutional structures to encourage and foster the Camelot debates necessary for our moral and political powers to overthrow the power of capital, these debates will never happen. That is why an incoming socialist administration must simultaneously chain Capital and legislate for the structural conditions to enable the indirect Camelot model of democracry to take off. If it does not address the need for a written constitution to enable a democracy which provides for more than the economic empowerment of agents, the administration is indulging in wishful thinking with whatever positive legislation it promotes. Reform of our democratic structures is an integral part of the business of replacing the aristocracy of capital with the authority of the good.

3. Empowerment and the layers of citizenship

I have suggested that the appropriate notion of empowerment

New Statesman and Society (2 December 1988) for a copy of the charter. Unlike 'Charter 88' I have not mentioned electoral reform. This is an enormous topic. I touch on it in §6 below.

that underlies the idea that democracy is concerned with the empowerment of people is a notion of empowerment concerned with the legislative structures that enable our Camelot debates. We cannot regain the direct Camelot model of democracy. We cannot regain the Athenian version of the indirect Camelot model. However, it is not beyond our reach to fashion a version of the indirect Camelot model fit for contemporary society. What is required is that at every layer of social and political life structures are guaranteed that make the re-emergence of our traditions of the good and the reference groups which carry those traditions possible.

Clearly there is something right about the thought that the larger the size of a polity the harder it is for its citizens to be empowered. Size and distance matter when setting up empowerment relations which make representatives accountable in more than the economic sense. This means that if our modern society is ever to achieve something that even approximates to the indirect Camelot model of democracy it will require that genuine political power be placed in those areas most accessible to the citizens. In other words, it must be an integral part of a socialist constitution that political power be located, whenever possible, at the local and regional levels in preference to the national level. This is not a particularly radical idea. The UK practice prior to the present sequence of Tory administrations exemplified, to a degree, just such a distribution of power. However, in recent years, the UK has seen the emasculation of local government and its subjugation to the will of the national government. This must be reversed.

It seems reasonable to suppose that the primary place at which empowerment occurs is within communities of a size to encourage face-to-face encounters. Such communities do not need detailed constitutions to enable genuine discourse about the good to occur. Such communities are able, in virtue of the closeness of contact, to foster reference groups and traditions of thought and feeling that support something close to the ideal of a Camelot-style debate. As long as these communities are not subjected to the disruptive effect of subjugation before the profit margins of capital, talk and action of the good will proceed. Saying this is not an unreasonable act of faith; it is simply realism about our deep-seated human need to find solace and agreement with our fellows. And if the only communities that currently fit this model are no more than the community of an atomic family, so be it. That simply shows the amount of work that needs be done to enable richer and wider notions of community to flourish.

We must then consider the secondary and tertiary areas of empowerment. What sorts of areas must be defined and protected within a written constitution? There are a number of obvious cases and we can plot them by considering two dimensions of abstraction from the primary source of empowerment; the family, neighbourhood, or whatever face-to-face communities are available within modern society. In the first place we can abstract from the primary source by considering communities of greater size. The second dimension of abstraction comes from considering communities which differ in purpose rather than mere size from the primary community.

Along the first dimension of abstraction the most important community will be local government, that level of government with control over the local environment and services that govern the quality of daily local life: refuse collection, amenities, etc. If history is a reliable witness we shall want a further level of government and empowerment between the local and national; we shall want a level of regional government with control over those aspects of social life that require, for a number of reasons, the flexibility of response in planning that can only come from dealing in sufficiently large numbers. The obvious examples from the UK experience are education and health administration. And for these places of empowerment, the local and regional levels of government, to succeed in enabling citizenship, their role in determining policy must be clearly defined and demarcated (and protected!) from national policy-making. For if the local and regional governments have their power denied them, so do the citizens for whom these arenas provide the immediate source of empowerment outside the family and neighbourhood.

Along the second dimension of abstraction the most obvious and important arena of empowerment is within the politics of the workplace. Our place of work and the people with whom and for whom we work are one of the most important arenas of social life. If our workplace is also to be an area in which we can develop our social life and find the opportunities to flourish, this too must come within the compass of our written constitution. That is, the freedom of association within our constitution must include the freedom to join, or not to join, a trade union. Furthermore the right of a union and the workforce in general to participate in the management of an industry must be secured if the workforce is not to suffer gross disempowerment. For remember, we are talking about more than economic empowerment, more than the right to leave one's post and scour the market for employment elsewhere. We are talking about the sort of empowerment that obtains when the management and its decisions are accountable to the workforce not just in terms of the workforce's ability to walk away from bad practices, but in terms of its ability to engage in the development of good practices and the critique and emendation of bad ones. For that to be possible, our constitution must lay down in detail the right relations and structures of control within and between unions and management.

Now, this may seem pretty unspectacular so far. What is so special about this requirement of a detailed written constitution governing the various layers of citizenship we have so hurriedly sketched? After all, all manner of politicians of varying political hues have taken up the call for a detailed Bill of Rights, so why the sudden appearance of this demand here within a book about socialism? Now, my aim is not to detail the specifics of a written constitution. That I leave to others. My concern, as ever, is only with outlining the appropriate conceptual map for a tenable version of socialism. However, I have hurriedly sketched the sorts of domain a Bill of Rights must traverse for an important reason. This is that I believe that a Bill of Rights as traditionally conceived only does half the job required. A Bill of Rights must lay out the abstract legal structure that needs to be in place for promotion of the good life, promotion of the authority of the good, to flourish. As indicated, it must define a number of different arenas of empowerment and accountability. Furthermore its central task must be to define the appropriate relations of association, control and influence between the various levels. The Bill of Rights must lay down the proper domain of local and regional government and mark out those areas over which national government may not interfere. This is no small task, but it needs to be done.[1] It is the task of detailing the structures required to integrate our various domains of empowerment. Note also the fact that we start with the family, perhaps also the neighbourhood, as the primary place of empowerment is not derived from some abstract dictum that small is beautiful. There is no *a priori* presumption in favour of the small. For all I know big may be pretty wonderful too. What does seem apparent is that, whatever size is appropriate, our various arenas of empowerment must be integrated. The relations between our different domains of social life must be well marked and regulated.

When all this legal structure is in place, however, it still lacks the key element which alone will turn it into a charter for the liberation of the good. As I have already said, the abstract concerns of a Bill of Rights must accompany a socialist administration's attempts to promote various non-market criteria of the good. Without the Bill of Rights, promotion of the authority of the good will fail through lack of the appropriate machinery for bringing people together in the image of the Camelot debate. But the converse is just as important. Without a systematic attempt to promote the good the abstract Bill of Rights is hollow. The legislative programme of an incoming socialist administration must do more than merely set a legal agenda for debate, it must have the courage of its convictions to take the lead in providing a charter for democracy that actively promotes not only the structure for debate about the good, but the good itself. And it is because I believe that a socialist administration must attempt so much that the concern for abstract issues about democracy has surfaced so late in my argument. Considered in the abstract they offer no more than the pluralistic economism about values typical of liberalism. A socialist constitution has more meat on it than that. It amounts to a full-blown charter for democracy which covers the content as well as the structure of our social life and the ensuing empowerment of citizens.

4. Empowerment: a charter for democracy

More than a Bill of Rights is required for the political

[1] See Paul Hirst's 'Associational socialism in a pluralist society', *Journal of Law and Society* (1988), 139-50, for an attempt along these lines with which I have some sympathy.

empowering of agents which lies at the heart of socialism. Along with the abstract legal framework typical of numerous Bills of Rights around the world and proposed in 'Charter 88', socialism has a more detailed and specific charter to offer. It is not enough merely to lay out the legal framework of a good society: we must provide a first specification of the content. What I mean by a charter for democracy does just that.

I want to develop this idea in the light of recent developments in educational reform in the UK. The 1988 Education Reform Act has done many things to the UK education system, much of it undoubtedly harmful. One proviso of the Act which incensed parents and educationalists from the outset was the provision for the testing of pupils at the ages of seven, eleven, fourteen and sixteen. In particular, much fury was aroused at the idea that children as young as seven would find themselves subjected to standardised testing, which seemed more concerned with the evaluation of teachers than enhancing the educational career of the pupil. There was much confusion in the proposals. For example, it was clear from the government consultation papers that they had not clearly distinguished the different roles that tests can play in education. Tests can be used to check whether children are learning. They can be used to moderate teacher performance within and between different schools, and they can be employed to diagnose a child's development and likely needs for future learning. It is not clear that these different roles can be served by one sort of test. This, however, is in the past. The government set up a working party to devise the appropriate tests and attainment levels to make their general demand work. The Task Group on Assessment Techniques (TGAT), chaired by Professor Black, has now reported and had the broad framework of its recommendations accepted by the Minister of State for Education. In the work of this report and its apparent acceptance by government a small miracle has occurred.[1] For the TGAT report is no less than a charter for good education that marks and promotes the very non-market criteria of excellence most people thought would be swamped by the outlines of the 1988 Education Act. It is this charter that

---

[1] Details of the report can be found in *National Curriculum: Task Group on Assessment and Testing: A Report*, Department of Education and Science and the Welsh Office (1988).

I wish to use as a model for the charter for democracy. Let me explain what has happened with the report on assessment in education.

The fear about the testing proposals was that they would amount to no more than standardised written tests which would set school against school in a scramble to be seen to be performing well on a league table of test results and which would thereby detract from the main business of educating young children. Worse still, the prospect that a child might be marked a failure at the age of seven raised spectres of discrimination that most people thought had been banished for good from the British education system. But in broad outline the TGAT report has succeeded in formulating a series of tests and attainment levels which side-step these fears and look set to produce much excellence. It has excelled in two main areas.

To begin with, it has for the first time codified teachers' expectations for children as they progress through the education system. It has laid down the sorts of skills, abilities and knowledge that a successful education system should be imparting. It has done this in considerable detail, specifying a series of achievements which can be expected of, for example, a typical seven-year-old. Now there is nothing new in the idea of having such expectations. All school teachers have within their own minds a series of expectations which they continually apply to the children in their care. First-rate teachers have always gone into a term, a week, and a class with expectations about what sorts of attainments they are aiming at for their children within the allotted time span. The achievement of the TGAT report has been to codify what gifted teachers have been doing all along to provide a uniform charter of excellence in teaching and curriculum development.

The second achievement of the TGAT report has been to develop methods of testing to see whether or not a given child is reaching the attainments expected. It has developed a system to enable teachers to diagnose those who need more attention and highlight the areas in which work is needed. This has been the most sensitive and difficult area of the report's work. What it has done is to develop a common language of appraisal that allows the attainment levels proposed to be used as a device for propelling children through their education to reach their full potential. The difficulty with assessment is this. It is all too easy to employ a common language of assessment which debases teaching. That is, if we set such and such a task as the norm for a seven-year-old, it is tempting to test the child along a range from success to failure. The result of the testing amounts to no more than a series of numbers, 4/10, 7/10, 5/10 etc. with some specified level designated as the pass/fail divide. But that tells us little of educational value. All it amounts to for any given child is a statement of that child's development with regard to a national norm. If a given child is either an early or late developer, such assessment methods give no useful information at all. What the TGAT report has proposed is something different.

The proposals for testing involve the development of a much more sophisticated method both of testing itself and of recording the results. On the former, the tests proposed for seven-year-olds are not written tests with simple right or wrong answers. Instead the intention is that children will be set tasks or project work, from a bank of topics, on which they may work for a week or more. The project will then be evaluated by the child's teacher and moderated within the school. The project will be interdisciplinary and provide the opportunity to evaluate a number of skills and abilities. Clearly, with such tests, a response such as '6/10' is wholly inappropriate. Instead, at the time of writing, much work is going on to develop a codified and moderated system of appraisal that will both be richer than the default option of 'pass/fail' and yet provide an objective indicator which is not merely a reflection of the subjective meaning that one particular teacher may give to the phrase 'Sound effort but could do better'! The work on developing such a codified system of appraisal is still being done. The central point of the proposals is that the result of an assessment on, say, a seven-year-old, is not to label the child with an achievement – pass, fail, 6/10 etc. Rather it is a measure of where the child is along a codified plan of achievement leading to development of her full potential. If at seven the child measures below the norm, that is not a failure: it is merely an indication of exactly what needs to be done to make that assessment out of date when the child is next tested. The whole process is geared as a dynamic evaluation, an aid to educational development.

Now I have outlined the work of the TGAT report at some

length, for not only is it intrinsically interesting but it serves as a model for the sort of charter for democracy that a socialist administration should seek to supply. That is, in addition to the formal legal requirements of a Bill of Rights, a socialist government should, as a matter of equal urgency, do for all its domains of operation what TGAT has done for testing and assessment in education. That is just the sort of thing I mean when I say that a socialist administration should be prepared to give the lead by commissioning research to lay down charters for excellence in health care, housing, education, welfare provision etc. It is not enough to lay down the bare legal bones of a Bill of Rights. Socialists must also be prepared to describe the recipe for the good, for it is only by providing the charters to ensure that the good in these central arenas is genuinely available universally that all people can be genuinely empowered within our polity. Only then do we achieve a democracy.

Of course, in providing specific charters for our social life we may, and probably will, get some things wrong. But that is not a reason for inaction, it is just a reminder of the responsibility we bear when engaged on such projects. Note also the following moral from the TGAT case. The TGAT report lays down various criteria for excellence in teaching and the assessment of children. For excellence to ensue these criteria must have priority. That is to say, if the resources are not made available to fund the recommendations of the report its work will have been wasted. Without the funds and time required to develop and employ a new common language of assessment, the worry must be that teachers will have no option but to fall back on the default option of a common language of appraisal: pass, fail, 6/10 etc.

The general moral then is this: there needs to be a charter for democracy outlining the detailed provisions necessary for the empowering of agents within our society in virtue of the legal framework in a Bill of Rights and the substantive needs in education, health etc, for achieving citizenship. And this charter must be given priority in forming government policy. Specifically, we outline the needs required by the charter and *then* fix the tax levels required to fund it. We do not determine first what tax levels look acceptable and then see how much of our charter can be accomplished. Our first aim is to provide a society shaped by moral values, not the forces of Capital. We must embrace this openly and place our charter for democracy firmly out in front as our first priority. And doing so is not necessarily electoral suicide, although we have become so used to the thought that it must be that most people think it inevitable. However, from the evidence of the annual British Social Attitude Surveys the numbers in favour of higher public spending at the expense of tax cuts has been rising, reaching 50 per cent in 1987. Anyway, there is much to the thought that the British electorate has yet to be presented with a clearly argued and well-defined policy programme of legitimate public spending and so claims about how it would or would not respond are largely untested. The writing of the charter for democracy is a first step to such a policy programme.

Clearly I cannot attempt to write the details of such a charter here. No one person has the expertise to undertake such a task, but the general need for such a thing has, I hope, been made plain.

5. Can the law be neutral?

My account of the placing of a Bill of Rights alongside a much more specific charter for democracy puts me at odds with a common account of the role and rule of law within a democracy. It is precisely because liberals are neutral about the good that they elevate the abstract requirements of something like a Bill of Rights to the sanctity of the rule of law. The law must be inviolable and stand above the tangled mess of our differing conceptions of the good. In contrast I have suggested that a socialist constitution will be incomplete if it does not involve a detailed charter for the good. This must complement the abstract structure of a Bill of Rights. But if this is right, the law cannot be neutral, it cannot be conceived as a fixed benchmark within which we argue about the good. Instead it must be seen as part of our continuing process of trying to formulate the good.

Such an account of the nature of law is available within contemporary jurisprudence. It has been articulated with eloquence in the work of Ronald Dworkin.[1] If the position I

---

[1] His major theoretical statement is to be found in *Law's Empire* (London &

have outlined is tenable we cannot distinguish between the law and our morals in a way that might leave the former an independent neutral judge on disagreement over the latter. Our law must be thought of as no more than the currently evolved attempt to write our charter for democracy. Now the substantial issues in the philosophy of law that underpin this conception of the relation between law and politics, or law and morals in general, are well outside the compass of this short book. However, I should mention one area which may look pressing. This concerns the question whether it is ever justifiable to break the law. For example, is civil disobedience ever justified?

One simple way of answering this question is to appeal to the distinction between constitutional law and those laws not part of a written constitution. We could then justify breaking the latter law if it could be shown that it was at odds with the written constitution. But if the law in general cannot be thought of as a fixed benchmark within which we argue about the good, this response is worthless. It fails to take account of the possibility that, at any point in time, the written constitution may itself be mistaken and the non-constitutional law, for example an interpretation of some statute fixed by a judge, may be the better guide. So let us change focus slightly.

Suppose the model of the law as an extension of our best attempts so far to write that charter for democracy is right. Consider now the question whether we can ever be justified in breaking the law as it exists. To this question the obvious answer must be that we are. For the prevailing conception and practice of the law in the UK is a conception that treats the law as a neutral arbiter over differing conceptions of the good. The practice is sometimes true to this and, more often, not. Much of our law is no more than a thinly disguised attempt to protect the status quo of property right distributions. This is a usual claim made by Marxist analyses of the law and made about the law in general. I am not making that claim, but I do think that the scope for critiques of components of our current law as ideological, in the sense noted in Chapter 3, is valid.[1] If socialists genuinely believe that the goal is to articulate a

Cambridge, Mass. 1986).

[1] For a good acccount of a Marxist analysis of the law see Hugh Collins, *Marxism and Law* (Oxford 1982).

conception of the good society enshrined within a charter for democracy as suggested, there can be no alternative honest answer to the question of the legitimacy of breaking current UK law than to admit that it can be legitimate. This is not to provide a determinate decision procedure for spotting the legitimate instances, it is only to admit that in principle the law as it stands is not sacrosanct.

Now suppose a different situation in which we have achieved something like the sort of socialist constitution I have suggested. In this case would civil disobedience ever be legitimate? The answer still has to be that it could be legitimate. The law is still not sacrosanct, but there is a difference and it matters. In commenting on discussions of civil disobedience Dworkin remarks:[1]

> It would make no sense to debate how far law should be obeyed if one side thought that the enactments of Parliament were the only source of law and the other side gave that power to the Bible. But if many people in the community disagreed that far about grounds – if they shared no paradigms at all – civil disobedience would be the least of their problems.

The point is this. If we achieved some agreement on a constitution containing a detailed charter for democracy, that is to suppose that we have a large degree of agreement available in terms of which particular instances of civil disobedience can be assessed. It is not to suppose that no such instances might arise, or that they might not sometimes be justified. It is just to note that a common framework would most likely be available for adjudicating any instance that did occur. But on the general question it leaves the possibility of legitimate law-breaking open. This is different from the situation where our law fails to enshrine much by way of common purpose, especially where it operates without a written constitution to guide at least on questions of procedure. My suspicion is that, at the present moment in the UK, we are somewhere between these two extremes. We are a long way from an agreed body of constitutional law, let alone a specific charter for democracy. And we are dangerously close to that breakdown of agreed standards of adjudication that renders

[1] Op. cit., 113.

civil disobedience the least of our problems. There is no doubt that for many of our society the option of acting outside the law looks to be the only course of action left open. And it does not follow from that that such actions are justified, but neither is it immediately apparent that they are not.

The point I am urging here is just this. If my account of what socialism is all about is right, we must admit that the failure of our present legal system to do much by way of encoding our conceptions of the good makes it a legitimate target for critique and leaves wide open the possibility that, on many issues, civil disobedience will be justifiable. For, at the end of the day, the justification of such action resides not in its conformity with some higher law, for example, the constitution, even if it were there. It resides in the conformity of the action with our best current attempt to articulate the authority of the good. Legal justification for action must defer to our moral justification. That might seem a hopelessly anarchistic call for chaos. It is not. It is the echo of the call for a written constitution and detailed charter for democracy which alone can provide the conditions for rendering civil disobedience an obsolescent mode of action.

Take an analogy that I have used before. Within a family we might ask if it is ever legitimate to disobey one's parents. But the very raising of the question only reveals the breakdown in what we might call the common charter of family life. That is not to suppose that parents have some absolute power over their offspring which should never be broken – far from it. It is only to note that in a family which understands its common purposes and has accepted ways of co-ordinating its plans and wishes, the question of the legitimacy of breaking parental authority hardly arises. Strip away its common plan and we are left with the abstract claims of authority and critiques of it. Then a family is in need of a charter for democracy. That is the need of our society today. And to admit that this leaves open the possibility of justified civil disobedience is not idealistic just because it has been, of late, unthinkable, let alone unsayable. If stated firmly and openly it would, I think, have many supporters. We know the law can be an ass, why not admit it? The fear of admitting it is the fear of having no hand rails left to guide our progress. But if we are afraid of *that*, civil disobedience is, as Dworkin says, the least of our problems.

Our need is for a durable set of hand rails: a Bill of Rights supplemented by a detailed charter for democracy.

6. Regulation for the good

In all this I have avoided the question of electoral reform. I have done this for two reasons. First, this is a need that is specific to particular countries and not a general theoretical need. What is of general importance is the need that our electoral systems be such as to provide for moral empowerment and the moral accountability proposed above. But the particular question of whether or not, for example, the present UK system does this is a matter peculiar to the UK.

Secondly, the question is diffuse and complicated, and discussion of it still in its infancy. People talk too glibly of proportional representation without bothering to distinguish the many different forms of voting systems that fall under that general category.[1] Also, all discussions of voting reform have taken place within a presumption in favour of the third, or polyarchical, model of democracy outlined above. The concern for reformers is to provide a system that reflects fairly the diversity of opinion within a community. But it is not obvious that that is the only constraint upon a system of voting. It should also be a system matched to the requirement of moral empowerment. For example, one way of ensuring the desirable accountability between national representatives and the electorate would be this. Rather than alter the system of voting, make the election of the national parliament a system of rotating elections as with UK local government, so that, for example, one third of the parliament stood for election every two years. If such a reform were in place, it is not so clear that the issue of simple majority first-past-the-post systems versus proportional representation systems would be such a live issue. Similarly, if we had a written constitution and a charter for democracry that outlined and guaranteed the duties of different levels of government and marked clearly the boundaries between them so that national government could

[1] Once more, for a general introduction to these topics a valuable source is McLean, op. cit., although I am unhappy with his preferences among PR systems, especially his requirement that a system should aim to pick the Condorcet winner.

not, for example, disable local government in the way that Tory administrations have done, once again it is unclear that the perceived need for electoral reform would be so great. In short, the debate about electoral reform focusses attention on the wrong issues. There is a question about the justice of our voting systems, but there are far more important questions about the point and structure of our democracy: the point of our having representatives at all, however they get elected. We need to address these matters urgently. We need our written constitution and charter of democracy to empower citizens. That is the first requirement. If we get it right, electoral reform may yet turn out to be a minor irritant.

The picture that emerges from this is a picture of a highly structured society in which a detailed written constitution guarantees the position of each and every member of society, their place and their access to the various domains of government power whether at the local, regional or national level. Some will find this picture uncongenial because of the detailed structure, but without this structure the possibility of achieving a society shaped by moral forces rather than the profit motive will not be available. It simply is not true that in practice capitalism and democracy cannot do without each other, whatever otherwise intelligent theorists may say.[1] It may well be true that, as a feature of recent history, democracies have arisen in those societies in which the economic freedom of the market has been a dominant force in the structure of society. But that is an historical point, not an analytic one, and there is probably a good reason for it too. For, in the historical situation of breaking free of the traditions and social structures of feudalism it was, perhaps, necessary for the achievement of political freedom that the bonds be broken by the rise of economic freedom. But having achieved some distance from the traditions of feudalism there is no a priori reason, or sound practical reason, why democracy, in more than the thin sense giving economic empowerment, should require the free market of capitalism. Ryan is also wrong when he remarks that, 'If the citizens of the Soviet bloc were allowed a free vote on their preferred economic system their choice

[1] See Alan Ryan's article on citizenship in *The Times* (25 October 1988) for just this remark.

would be private ownership and free enterprise.'[1] This has not been the call of the dissident groups within the Soviet Union or, for that matter, the call of the banned Polish trade union Solidarity. Although it is clear that the members of such states envy the ready availability of consumer goods in western countries, it is far from clear that we must defer to an iron law of history that states that we can not form democracies and substantive charters for democracy without also embracing capitalism and the free market. We are not constrained like that. The shape of our social world is, in part, of our own making. We can do with it as we will. With courage we can overcome the requirements of Capital and replace them, through our charters for democracy, with the requirements of the good. After all, the very term 'capitalism' has been with us only since the 1860s.[2] There is no requirement that we must stick with it for ever.

---

[1] Ibid.

[2] E. Hobsbawm, *The Age of Capital 1848-1875* (London 1975), 13.

7

The Lion and the Unicorn:
the peculiarities of English socialism

The heirs of Nelson and of Cromwell are not in the House of Lords. They are in the fields and the streets, in the factories and the armed forces, in the four-ale bar and the surburban back garden; and at present they are still kept under by a generation of ghosts.

(George Orwell, *The Lion and the Unicorn*, 1941)

1. The heritage

To write a book on socialism without mentioning the concept of class is perhaps strange. To write a book on socialism from within English political experience and not mention the concept of class is surely plain carelessness.[1] The English class system is one of the major peculiarities of life on this island. It is the feature of social life guaranteed to disarm and disorient a foreigner coming to live here. The unwritten codes of dress, housing, manner, whom one should talk to and what niceties of introduction must be effected before one is so bold as to make conversation even with those of an accessible class – all these are matters that permeate English life and make for an unwritten agenda to confuse and confound the outsider. The

[1] I deliberately limit my discussion to the English experience, rather than the Welsh, Scottish or Irish. As someone who has lived and taught in Scotland, I am only too well aware of the vast difference in culture and social life between England and Scotland. North of the border, I am pleased to report, there is still a strong sense of community traditions that hold social life together and act as a bulwark against the forces of Capital. There is an openness to social intercourse that rings strange but refreshing to anyone brought up in the south. To a lesser degree, a similar point holds when contrasting the North/South divide within England.

English class system is important, but not in the way many think.

We must distinguish between two notions of class. In the first place there is the theoretical concept of class familiar in political theory from Marx's theory of history. This is the concept of social classes defined in terms of their economic position with regard to Capital and which, in terms of Marx's theory, are necessarily thrown into conflict with one another. This is the theory of history as the progression of class warfare. This concept of class has not been, and is not, important in my account of socialism. I have not employed and do not endorse the materialist theory of history. Nor do I believe that such an economic concept of class can much affect, or be much employed within, the sorts of arguments that I have deployed in this book. Indeed within the framework of my argument the only relevant structural economic concept of class division is this: the distinction between those who serve and identify with the interests of Capital and those who do not. However, whether or not you call the former the capitalists and the latter the proletariat is of little moment. For the latter class is a vast and varied collection with no homogeneous character. Now although it has been a key idea to my argument that we should act so as to develop non-capitalist criteria of social organisation and development, I have done this through the concept of the reference group. This is a smaller social grouping than the rambling class of all those who do not identify with the interests of Capital. Being a member of the class of those who do not identify with the interests of Capital is not something that impinges on our consciousness and our behaviour. Being a teacher, being a nurse, being a small businessman, being a childminder, a plumber, a cook, a member of a church, a parent, a black person or a woman – these are groupings in our social life which engage with our purposes and stratagems. These are the groupings that matter to what we do and how we act and the principles and values that shape these actions. And it is from such smaller and, from the point of view of our moral purpose in life, more salient groupings that we must define our opposition to the interests of Capital. Being a member of the class of those who do not serve the interests of Capital is simply not a salient feature of my life nor the life of many, if of any at all.

Of course, this is not to deny that in the nineteenth century membership of this economic class may have been a salient feature of social life, or at least more relevant than today. That is not ruled out. And of course part of the explanation of the failure of Marx's prediction of Communist revolution in the industrial nations lies in the way that the significance of membership of this class has come to shrink in so far as membership impinges upon an individual's plans of action. Improvements in the condition of the working class have weakened the importance of membership of this economically defined class in thinking about social and moral purpose. What has not weakened is the way the more ancient English class system has continued to structure social life.

The concept of class that figures in the notion of the 'English class system' is not an economically defined notion of class. It is a different concept and a more powerful one. It is, essentially, a cultural concept. It is a concept of class that provides class distinctions that cut across the distinctions provided by economic class divisions. It is a notion of class that reaches far back in our common consciousness and that continues ancient feudal and medieval divisions in our society. Why this should be so in this small island I do not know. But the sense of class differences which, to anyone brought up in this country, is tangible in a myriad different ways has more in common with the caste system of India than with the economic divisions of Marxist theory. The differences we feel and react to are differences in dress, accent, style of housing and diet, typical recreations and places of schooling. Unlike American society, where social elevation is very much a function of business success, or French society, where social elevation is more closely related to simple meritocratic notions, in England social success is still very much a function of class. This, of course, is the reason why, among certain regions of the Tory party, the dominance of a grocer's daughter has been such a painful experience.[1]

In short, the English class system is very much to do with the shadow of feudal traditions that have lingered on into the industrial age and still dominate the structure of our society.

---

[1]And who knows to what extent Mrs Thatcher's macho agressiveness is a function of her perception of the class distinctions she has trampled across?

Our problem is very much that of learning to supplant these traditions with new ones fit for the modern age. The heirs of Nelson and Cromwell are kept under by generations of feudal ghosts. What is wrong with this?

As ever, I do not think that the problem with the English class system is that it is inequitable, that it encourages unfair distribution of goods and services in society, though no doubt that is true. We only have to look at the way the private education sector continues to dominate both Oxbridge entrance and, through that, the higher reaches of the civil service to see the truth in this remark. In itself, inequity in distribution does not matter. The failing of the English class system goes deeper than that.

In a healthy society, a morally fit society, individuals will find their moral and political purpose mapped out through the various reference groups they inhabit and the traditions thereby supplied. But, as argued earlier, these reference groups and their traditions must be open-ended to avoid a charge of ideology. There must be no closed barriers between traditions. The healthy society is an integrated society. As I argued in the last chapter, the only way to ensure this is to provide a detailed written constitution not only detailing a formal legal structure, but providing also a charter for democracy which sets down the criteria for flourishing in key areas of our social life. The problem with the English class system is that it systematically obstructs this integration. It provides keenly felt and, generally, closely observed demarcation lines between the different reference groups in our society. It ensures that ours is a fragmented society.

There is a sense in which the English class system has been of much value, for it has, until very recently, acted as a bulwark against the total destruction of our moral traditions by the forces of Capital. Our class system has provided some comforts against the cold chill of the free market, for it has encouraged the preservation of limited traditions and reference groups. One's position in society may be largely a function of one's birth, but at least one can achieve some comfort within the solidarity of one's class. But the price of this has been the promulgation of moral traditions that provide at best a blinkered view of society and encourage the fragmentation of English society into a hierarchy of societies.

This is terribly convenient for those who can then block out the fate of others from a lower class. For example, the quality of life of the long-term unemployed surviving on mean welfare benefits does not touch the life of those for whom the path from cradle to achievement is strewn only with encouragement, useful contacts and gilt-edged handshakes. After all, from the point of view of the privileged classes, those for whom success, wealth and graceful living are a birthright, the degradation of the unemployed takes place in a different country. They live in different places, in state-owned housing; they go to different pubs; they seek out different entertainments; they walk different streets and drive different cars; they look mean and hungry, and they struggle in different schools and languish in different hospitals. The English class system's failure consists in the systematic way it allows us to forget those who occupy these different lands and who fight for a life in different places. It packages our concerns for those like ourselves. That is natural. What is unnatural is the rigidity of the packaging, the block to any further integration between our different reference groups, the fixed demarcation lines of concern. And it does not matter how often you read accounts of what it is like to live in the 1980s on Income Support,[1] for as long as you are reading of the lives of those who, due to the class divisions in our society, constitute a different nation there is no framework for the natural concern for a fellow human being to develop and encompass.

The problem for the English Left is to articulate frames of reference that not only replace the logic of Capital but shatter the packaging of the English class system. It is the problem of reviving a lost political culture, a shattered notion of what a civil society might look like. It is, as much as anything, a problem about finding the right language in which to address questions of distribution of goods and services. There is much we can learn here from Europe where moral traditions survive in healthier conditions than at home and where they are, relative to the English experience, untrammelled by the vagaries of class. And the problem for the Left is now exacerbated by the way that the Thatcher regimes have opened

---

[1] See B. Campbell, *Wigan Pier Revisited* (London 1984) or the report in the *Guardian* (14 December 1988), p. 21 about life on Income Support on a Glaswegian council estate.

up the divisions of the class system for the benefit of Capital to run free. There is a danger of conflating two separate critiques of the Thatcher free-market experiment. We criticise it not to return to the security of the class-ridden status quo, for, although that may offer frames of reference and traditions that give some shape to social life, it offers only ideologically blinkered and packaged frames of reference. It does not offer the scope for an integrated social life where our traditions are free from the charge of ideological closure.

Our task then is to redefine our civil society. We have to shake off the constraints of our class system and, with our charters for democracy, refashion our communities within an integrated society in which it is not unnatural to be moved by the plight of those for whom any future at all, let alone one in which they flourish, is something that only happens to others. There are various key domains in which we must act and break up the hegemony of Capital and the heritage of our class system.

2. The economy

I remarked in Chapter 2 that my argument there offered the prospect of profitable alliances between the owners of small businesses and a socialist party. Such alliances come naturally in Italy, but here they are forbidden by the demarcation lines of class. This has to be changed.

The prospect for alliance resides in the following fact. The conditions for successful agency in the domain of many small businesses are not the same as the conditions for successful agency for big business. The latter, generally, profit from the deregulation of financial markets and the freedom to transfer Capital and money across national borders. Indeed, for the multinational corporations that so dominate our economy, such deregulation and freedom is essential. It does not even matter to such large corporations if the foreign exchanges are volatile. For such businesses there is money to be made by diversifying into currency speculation; and, for the shrewd operator, the prospect of moving significant amounts of money around the foreign exchanges can compensate for export difficulties within one small area of its operation. Things are different for the small specialist business. The conditions of successful agency for such concerns are not identical with the

conditions of Capital's success. Such businesses need an
economic space in which to breathe and to develop products.
They need a certain amount of security from the often hostile
winds of deregulated financial markets.

A good example of this need lies in the area of investment. A
comparison is often made between the different banking
practices in the UK and some of its major competitors, West
Germany being a good example. The difference is this. In the
UK the banks are not geared to long-term investment
strategies in a way that is common in West Germany. UK
banks are much more likely to take a short-term view and
assess a loan request with regard to how much return can be
expected this year or next in order to pay a good dividend in the
immediate future to its shareholders. This is not so in West
Germany. There it is much more common to engage a bank in
the sort of long-term financing which is so often essential for
the development of new products. It is a familiar anecdote
about English industrial life that our ability to come up with
new product ideas is matched only by our inability to find ways
of financing their development, with the consequence that the
new products end up being exported to a foreign manufacturer
to develop. There is much more than a grain of truth in such
anecdotes.

An important consequence of the attitudes of West German
banks is that the West German stock market is not nearly so
important to economic life as the UK stock market, for German
firms do not need share issues to raise capital for investment:
they get it from their banks. A consequence of this is to dampen
the game-like enthusiasm with which English companies play
the stock market looking for keen take-over bids and, once
more, unsettling the smooth economic and financial planning
so essential for a healthy small-business sector.

The German experience here is rather special, for the
attitude of their banking system to investment is not
something that has been imposed by state regulation. It has
simply arisen, naturally, out of different traditions. No doubt,
once again, the fact that the UK banking system has not
evolved like this is tied up with the class system. Banking is an
occupation that has typically been recruited from a different
class from that from which the engineers and manufacturing
leaders have come. When engineering friends complain that

their companies are run by accountants with a fine head for figures but an empty space where grasp of the needs of manufacturing should be, they are often enough voicing a class-based complaint. This is familiar; we should act to change it. No socialist party can afford to ignore the business community; no socialist party with the courage to throw off the shackles of an outmoded class sensibility has any good reason for ignoring the needs of large sections of our business community.

And there is plenty of scope for change here. The state can act to modify banking practices. One obvious route would be the creation of a state investment bank. But the state can do much to encourage the small business community, with which socialists have much common purpose in thwarting the unfettered profit motives of deregulated Capital. In a recent study it has been claimed that capitalist development is inherently neutral on the question of the optimum size of the firm. What matters is 'the way in which states, in pursuit of their own objectives, have inserted themselves in the economic process'.[1] Weiss's study of the importance of the small business sector in the Italian economy is of great importance. Despite the widespread identification of preferential treatment for small enterprises with the Thatcher regimes, Weiss is surely right to insist that the problems with the British small-business sector (the smallest in the developed capitalist world) centre on the 'incongruity of means (regeneration of small enterprise) and ends (extension of market principles).'[2] The Thatcher government's attitude to small business has been bound up with a philosophical task of ridding the country of collectivism and maximising market mechanisms. But, as Weiss concludes from her study of the Italian economy,[3]

> a small business solution is not an individualistic or market solution ... securing it requires a good deal of intervention from above and, one might add, a considerable degree of 'collectivism' from below.

[1] Linda Weiss, *Creating Capitalism: the state and small business since 1945* (Oxford 1988), 1.
[2] Ibid., 208.
[3] Ibid., 209.

An English socialist party must find the nerve to embrace the small-business community. It can only do this by cutting through the feudal hangovers of the class system. And note that in doing this it is not capitulating to Capital. It is seeking alliances with some capitalists, in the sense of those who own the means of production; but, as I argued in Chapter 2, ownership itself is not what matters. What matters is the capitalist and the notion of capitalism in the sense of those who favour that arrangement of society that favours the interests of Capital. That arrangement is the free market. As Weiss argues, capitalism (and she uses the term in the ownership sense) is neutral with regard to the forms of business, specifically size, that may develop. But capitalism, in the sense that I have been arguing against, is not neutral. I have been arguing against that conception of capitalism which takes the structural needs of Capital as primary in the organisation of society and that requires a free market and a drive to ever larger corporations. The important point is this: There is scope for much regulation of the market and dethronement of the needs of Capital without upsetting the economy of small enterprises. Indeed we can encourage such enterprises and still tear down the free-market façade that dislocates our social life. The choice is not a straightforward one between advancing the conditions of moral and political agency over and above the conditions of economic agency, for it all depends on how we construe the latter. Where we think of economic agency solely in terms of acting for the advancement of Capital, we must be opposed to it. That is how I have been using the term 'economic agency'. But there are kinds of economic agency within modern industrial society which defer to criteria other than the advancement of Capital. There is the agency of small enterprises. We can act to supplant the conditions of economic agency with the conditions of moral and political agency, but we do not thereby throw all economics out of the window. There is much scope for a new political economy which outlines the conditions of forms of economic agency other than those that defer to Capital and the free market. Weiss's study is a good starting point. Socialists must pick this up.

We have been too much impressed by Fordism in industrial life, which identifies the needs of the firm with the structural needs of Capital. The social damage caused in the name of the

Fordist advancement of big business and mammoth-scale production is familiar. The notion of 'post-Fordism' is becoming popular in media discussions of society. The simple point I want to press here is that embracing post-Fordist methods of production can, when we see the issues in political economy aright, be done without turning our backs on the economy and its needs altogether.

3. Education, health and other services

I have used the field of education and, to a lesser extent, that of the health services as examples throughout the argument of this book. The central need I have argued for in these areas is for a socialist party to articulate clearly the non-market criteria of success in these domains. This should be encapsulated within what I have called our charters for democracy. Having done that, a socialist party must promote these non-market criteria of success over and above the market-dominated mechanisms currently being put into play within the key services of English society.

A socialist party must formulate a clear alternative vision of, for example, education to oppose the 1988 Education Reform Act. As I remarked in the last chapter, some features of that Act are of great value, even if this is more an accident of government policy than conscious design. The general effect of the last ten years of Tory administration has been the subjugation of one area of social life after another by market criteria of success. This was made easier by the lack of any clear sense of an alternative set of criteria. Services have been allowed to run on an ad hoc basis and have thereby become easy prey to a government with a clear vision of how to structure educational supply. The fact that the chosen method of organisation turns out to have been pursued in unawareness of our best accounts of the way education works and of its needs is obscured by the fact that we currently lack a co-ordinated effort, or indeed a will, to write and promote a charter for educational excellence. As with all areas of social life concerned with providing a service for the community – health, housing, welfare, the environment – education is too precious to be left either to the market or to an ad hoc piecemeal grasp of what is required. What is required is the best account of the criteria of success we can furnish, and to produce that we must be clear what the criteria are and how to evaluate them once formulated. In short, we need to engage Camelot-style debates about the good in education, health, the environment and the other key domains. We should not be shy of doing this, we should not be reticent. We must start speaking of the good and promoting the good. Of course we will get things wrong. But that is far better than leaving the supply of these services to the fickle command of the market and the dethronement of any relevant notions of non-market goods altogether. Our reticence here is marked.

In part our reticence is again a function of our class sensibilities. For example, the arrangements that had arisen in a more or less ad hoc way for financing higher education bore all the hallmarks of an entrenched class system. That might seem a wholly uncharitable remark. After all, the Robbins report stated that higher education was the right of everyone with A-level success. But although such statements of principle have influenced the development of higher education in the period to the end of the 1970s, it is not at all clear that they have shaped a co-ordinated response to the cuts which have decimated our university system since then. The cries and wails that have filled senior common rooms in all our universities have sounded too much like the cries of vested interest. The complaints have been too much the complaints of those longing for a return to the status quo. They have rarely been principled complaints articulating a concern for a genuinely open system of university education in which access is guaranteed to all who are able to benefit. The complaint has too often been: 'We have lost x number of posts', or 'We are having to keep up our research profiles with an increasing teaching load'. Seldom has the complaint been that the actions of government are destroying the centres of culture and learning which are the birthright of all.

Academics have complained that the government does not value education for its own sake. But it is not clear that the government with its market-oriented obsession with crass and foolish criteria of efficiency and concentration upon vocational training is merely adopting a philistine approach. For the sons and daughters of Cabinet ministers do not, by and large, read for degrees in engineering and accountancy. They read the

classics, or history, or even philosophy, but these are not to be
generally available. The responses of the universities have
generally missed the point that the government is merely
reaffirming longstanding class hostilities. The government
does not dislike education *per se*, but it does not like too much
of it. This is where the universities have gone wrong. On those
occasions when they have championed the intrinsic value of
education for its own sake, they have done so without
encompassing this within a charter for democracy in
education. They have not come out and clearly stated their
enthusiasm for the intrinsic value of education as the
birthright of all. Until we get a clear charter of educational
excellence, we stand to get only the whinings of a class with
vested interests and not the interests of society at large. It is
an unfortunate side-effect of our heritage that those centres of
excellence in the university sector happen also to have been
bastions of privilege and playgrounds for the idle rich.
Oxbridge has done much to mend its ways in this respect. But
now, thrown to the crass insensitivities of the market, they
have taken to doing the government's work of privatisation for
it. Oxford has now launched its much publicised appeal for
funds to preserve its enormous intellectual heritage. But it has
appealed to the wrong people. With increased private funding
and greater selectivity of research focussed on 'useful' work,
once student vouchers and loans replace the grant system it is
more likely than not that Oxford will revert to its old status.
The vast majority of students able to afford loans for study will
be those for whom Oxford serves merely as a rite of passage
from public school to the higher echelons of the civil service. It
will still serve nicely as a backdrop for films about Hooray
Henrys and dons in quirky hats and fancy dress, but it will no
longer be one of the jewels in the crown of an internationally
renowned university system. The appeal that should have
happened was to the electorate at large: an appeal to
politicians and the media to tell people of our implicit charter
for educational excellence that still guides the work of
academics. It should have been an appeal for education against
the ravages of the market: an appeal that marked out the
non-market criteria of excellence in higher education – an
appeal that made plain to everyone that what is at stake is
their collective cultural and intellectual heritage, and not just

an institution for teaching upwardly-mobile youngsters the right way to talk and how to tell a claret from a burgundy.

If we want our universities to be more than expensive finishing schools for the privileged and well-off, we must be clear not only that university education is a good in itself, but that it is not just a good for a certain class. Remember, the government has not actually sanctioned the closing down of the university system, it has merely wanted to contract it. And until the point of that sector is seen clearly as something available for all irrespective of class and ability to pay, the complaints of senior common rooms will be easily ignored by the majority as the whimperings of privileged vested interests. Whether by design or accident, too much of our education system still mirrors our class divisions. As in the economic sphere, our charter for democracy in the educational sphere must break down the packaging of educational provision fostered by our inherited class obsessions.

Similar remarks apply to health and other social services. By a clever use of market forces, the government has sought to contract the amount and quality of health care available as a matter of right. The class divisions which always existed in our hospitals with private wards and pay-beds have been accentuated by holding our hospitals hostage to market criteria of efficiency. Once again, it is not that the government does not value health care; but by subordinating the management of its supply to market mechanisms it has succeeded in rationing a common need and right along traditional class divisions. And our problem here is not just that of reaffirming the criteria of excellence in health care over and above the market criteria of health supply. It lies as much in breaking our inherited acceptance of hierarchical divisions within our social life based upon our obsessive deference to class.

Opposition to the Thatcher government has been too timid. The opposition parties and the electorate at large have disliked what has happened within various isolated domains of our society – in health, in education, in care for the environment – but by and large the opposition has lacked the nerve and/or the theoretical resources to call for an alternative. The silence has been deafening as the government has repeatedly laid waste one arena after another and unleashed the power of market forces upon education, health and now the media. In each case opposition parties have been ready to cry that it is not fair; but this is a pathetic response. The correct response is to say that it is not good, for we have a better vision of what good education, health care and media provision look like. And the response must not be buffeted by the foolish moanings of curtailment of freedoms when the state acts to regulate education, health, the media etc. If the good is to flourish in these areas, they must be regulated. The freedom to have our news dictated by the megalomaniacs who currently control vast tracts of our media output debases the freedoms that matter and that can only come from within a clear vision of the criteria of what is good and flourishing within our social life.

However, among our opposition parties at least, we have lost the confidence to speak out for the non-market criteria of agency. We have lost the confidence to admit that the market is not the foolproof method of social organisation that those in command believe it to be. If the legitimation for interference that I have offered is correct, that confidence can and must be restored. We need no longer defer to the market and try only to tinker with its operation to gain whatever concessions from Capital that may from time to time be available. Instead we can make the market and the needs of Capital defer to *us*, to our lives, to our purposes. We can make it defer to our needs in education, health, the environment, the power industry and the media. There is little time left for this while the current disruption goes on apace. But we have the theoretical licence to call a halt and put an end to this foolish waste of human and social life and reaffirm the authority of the good over the aristocracy of capital.

4. An English socialist party?

Who, if anyone, is fit to take on the task of providing us with the necessary charters for democracy? Who is fit to reaffirm the authority of the good over the aristocracy of Capital? The likeliest candidate is the Labour Party, but they have a great deal to do to become fit for the role. It simply is not clear that they currently see the seriousness of the problem and the size of the task at hand. The alternative of forming a new socialist party hardly looks promising, although it must be the default option if Labour fails. If they do fail it will be because, trapped within dreary traditions of unionised vested interests, they will treat the problem as simply a technical matter of putting together sufficient votes to dethrone the Tories.

The problem for the English Left is not a technical problem. It is the problem of reviving a lost political culture, a shattered notion of what a civil society might look like. It is, as much as anything, a problem about finding the right language in which to address questions of distribution of goods and services. If we want help in learning how to define this culture there are some clues in that arena in which no British politician has ever felt genuinely at home: Europe. Europe may offer few utopias, but it is seldom as ravaged as our own political culture by the barbarisms of capitalism.

Consider the destruction already done at home. Ours is a barren political culture in which fear and bribery call the tune. It is bribery that keeps Mrs Thatcher in power afloat on a tide of rampant consumerism and unbridled egotism. In this moral vacuum of government-sanctioned gluttony ordinary households now run their finances to a Latin American rhythm – re-scheduling their debts every few months, nesting one loan within another like so many Russian dolls. It is bribery that fuels single-union deals and tears apart the *ancien régime* of union solidarity. And it is bribery that lures the potentially ill with the glossy brochures of hotels for the sick away from civil contact with the actually ill who suffer the ever-decrepit state hospitals.

Our society is not a civil one. It is not civility that bonds neighbours caught in a city street late at night. It is not civility that touches claimant and social security staff across the strengthened glass screen of the interview cubicle. It is not civility that informs our newspaper proprietors in the promotion of salacious gossip and half-baked innuendo that passes for reportage in so much of our 'free press'. It is fear that holds such barbarisms in place, the fear of losing whatever precious foothold in society we may have achieved, no matter how humble or elevated.

According to the Thatcherite vision, the route out of this fear lies within the grasp of each individual's moral consciousness. We only have to exercise enterprise in forging our contracts and bonds to escape the darkness. Jerusalem will be built upon

the shifting sands of contracts and bargains struck between
self-interested individuals operating in an otherwise moral
vacuum. Such an unimaginative and naïve vision would be
laughable if it were not, currently, so powerful.

What then is missing? The short answer I have proposed is
this: we have lost altogether the idea of a civil society, the idea
of citizenship that comes from finding our place within
integrated moral traditions rather than grasping a place
within a moral free-for-all. We have lost those traditions of
thought and feeling that help us to define our place and our
obligations and commitments within the communities in which
we live. Indeed, at root, we have lost our communities.
Notwithstanding Thatcher's strident rhetoric, even that
smallest of social groupings, the family, has begun to fall apart
under the self-interested pursuit of profit and economic
survival. The disruption of our political, civil and, finally,
familial traditions will be a fitting memorial to the Thatcher
years. And although deep-rooted historical inhibitions render
the idea of European solidarity anathema to many, it is in
Europe that we can still find traces of the political and civil
traditions we seem to have so totally abandoned.

After the release of the French hostages from Lebanon[1] a
French acquaintance remarked that, despite the obvious
dangers of the French government's policy, there was virtue in
whatever deal was struck. The virtue was that of the return of
a citizen to his home – not to his domestic home, but to the
larger home, the domain in which he was a citizen. Whatever
we think about that particular affair, or about the French in
general, the sentiment of citizenry is one that sits awkwardly
on the English tongue. Our inarticulation here is an
impoverishment.

Part of our problem lies, of course, in the outdated traditions
(including our class divisions) which, until recently, worked
tolerably well. Labour's dependence on the block votes of white,
male working-class unions, while inevitable at the birth of a
viable British Left, is now, frankly, an embarrassment, as is
also the continuing refusal of the party to forge adequate links
with its natural allies in the new social movements: for
example, the black sections. The Italian Communists, to take a

[1] July 1988.

familiar example, do not suffer from the same class impediments as our own Labour party. Nor does Mitterand's *Parti Socialiste.*

In contrast Thatcher has come dangerously close to eradicating the sense of civility and community that is the only real grounding for morally informed debate. She has come close to emptying social life of moral values and leaving us only with the catcalls of brokers and advertisers as we are enjoined to buy our way out of the dark quietude of uncivility.

The barbarians are in control, subjecting the last traces of civility to Capital's command for the maximisation of profit above all else. This neanderthal creed now demands that even schools and universities be run like mini-factories, with head teachers and vice-principals reduced to petty managers chasing nonsensical criteria of efficiency.

Whether or not Labour can revitalise the traditions of thought and feeling necessary to inform a truly civil society, it could make a start by looking at our European allies. The prospect of a socialist Europe might yet fire a second European renaissance. Apart from easing the stand against the capitalist giants of Japan and the US it would have the bonus of thoroughly irritating Mrs Thatcher who, judging from her recent bouts with Jacques Delors, is clearly afraid of Europe. For the Left to put its sights more firmly on Europe and its traditions of civility would, in itself, be a thorn in the Prime Minister's side.

If Labour is to be the socialist party that rids us of the Satanic mill of capitalism there are a number of things that it must do. First, it must learn to articulate its programmes within a central vision of a return to a society shaped by moral values not market forces. It must learn to engage the Camelot debates. Secondly, in doing this it must shake off its own class-based loyalties, give up its obsession with advertising its cloth-capped heritage, and write charters for democracy that provide an integrated opposition to Capital. Thirdly, it must forge alliances within the business community with those who, by no stretch of the imagination, can be termed agents of Capital. And if parts of Labour's union backing cannot stomach such alliances, Labour must learn to become what it has never been, a socialist party concerned for the social foundations of the good, not a party for organised labour. In doing this,

Labour must learn to break with its producer-side protectionism and distrust of Europe and look for a wider European alliance against Capital. If all this turns out to be heretical, socialists will have no option but to replace Labour with a genuine socialist party. The options here do not look favourable in the light of the pathetic scramblings in the centre ground of UK politics over the last few years. Whether that was a function of the intrinsic shallowness of what the centre alliance offered, or the practical difficulties of forming a new political party in this country at this time, only time will tell – if, that is, Labour fails to answer the needs for socialism: the need for the reconstruction of our social life.[1]

5. Taking charge of our world

Of course, it will be said that I have lost contact with the real world. In the real world first we must pay our way before we can start the reconstruction of social life. We must defer to the conditions of economic agency and get them right before we can afford to consider the conditions of moral agency. This is wrong. As I have argued, we do not need to turn our back on the needs of the economy to effect the changes required for socialism. We need only turn our back on the needs of Capital. And if most political economy fails to see the room for a distinction here, so much the worse for it. There is no reason, only blind habit, for accepting the priority of the conditions of free-market economic agency over those of moral agency. Of course we must pay our way in the world, but it is *our* world, and it is for us to decide what counts as paying our way. It is for us, not the bankers and accountants, or the merchants and the money lenders, to fix the priorities in favour of Capital. If we so choose we can fix the priorities the other way about. We can set the conditions of human life over those of the requirements of Capital.

It is our world we are fixing. It is for us to make good. We can choose to make the good come about. We can choose to set the agenda, to avoid the economism of the merchants of doom, and to fashion the conditions for individual and social human life to

---

[1] But note that Mitterand turned a shrunken and defunct socialist party into a party of government within years.

flourish. We do not have to languish before the money pots of Capital. We do not have to accept the agenda which blots out the authority of the good. We can, with nerve and determination, strike a new agenda and cast out the barbarians. If we do so we may well create anew the conditions of civility and virtue within our polity. Nothing is guaranteed. But by whatever name you call it, this Jerusalem, this Albion, this socialism is within our grasp.

Bibliography

Bacon, R., see Eltis & Bacon

Barry, B., 'Socialism today', Inaugural Lecture delivered at the London School of Economics, 3 December 1987

Berlin, I., 'Two concepts of liberty', in his *Four Essays on Liberty*, Oxford 1969

Bloom, A., *The Closing of the American Mind*, New York 1987 & London 1988

Bobbio, N., *The Future of Democracy*, ed. R. Bellamy, translated by R. Griffin, Cambridge 1987

Brown, A., *Modern Political Philosophy*, Harmondsworth 1986

Brubaker, R., *The Limits of Rationality*, London 1984

Campbell, B., *Wigan Pier Revisited*, London 1984

Child, J., *Organization*, New York 1984

Cohen, G., 'The labour theory of value and the concept of exploitation', *Philosophy & Public Affairs*, 1979

——, *Karl Marx's Theory of History: a defence*, Oxford 1978

——, 'Functional explanation, consequence explanation and marxism', *Inquiry*, 1982

Collins, H., *Marxism and Law*, Oxford 1982

Cripps, F. et al., *Manifesto*, London 1979

Dahl, R., *A Preface to Democratic Theory*, Chicago 1956

Dunn, J., *Western Political Theory in the Face of the Future*, Cambridge 1979

Dworkin, R., *Law's Empire*, London & Cambridge, Mass. 1986

Elster, J., 'Marxism, functionalism and game theory', *Theory and Society*, 1982

——, *Making Sense of Marx*, Cambridge 1985

Eltis, W. & Bacon, R., *Britain's Economic Problem*, Basingstoke 1976

Forbes, I., *Market Socialism: whose choice?*, Fabian Society pamphlet no. 516, London 1986

Gilder, G., *Wealth and Poverty*, New York 1981

Gould, B., *Freedom and Socialism*, Basingstoke 1985

Green, F. & Sutcliffe, B., *The Profit System: the economics of capitalism*, London 1987

Hackman, J. & Oldham, G., *Work Redesign*, Reading, Mass 1980

Hattersley, R., *Freedom and Choice*, London 1987

Held, D., *Models of Democracy*, Oxford & Cambridge 1987

Hirst, P., 'Associational socialism in a pluralist society', *Journal of Law and Society*, 1988

Hobsbawm, E., *The Age of Capital 1848-1875*, London 1975

Lively, J., *Democracy*, Oxford 1975

Luntley, M., *Language, Logic and Experience*, London 1988

——, 'The transcendental grounds of meaning' in *Scepticism and Meaning*, ed. K. Puhl, Berlin & New York, forthcoming

——, 'Bringing the state back in', *Political Quarterly* 1989

——, 'On the way the world is independent of the way we take it to be', *Inquiry*, 1989

Lukes, S., *Marxism and Morality*, Oxford 1985

MacIntyre, A., *After Virtue*, London 1981

McLean, I., *Public Choice: an introduction*, Oxford 1987

Macallum, R., 'Negative and positive freedom', *Philosophical Review*, 1967

Mackie, J., *Ethics: inventing right and wrong*, London 1978

Marx, K., *Economic and Philosophic Manuscripts 1844*, London 1973

Nozick, R., *Anarchy, State and Utopia*, Oxford 1975

Offe, C, *Disorganized Capitalism*, Oxford 1986

Oldham, G., see Hackman & Oldham

Orwell, G., *The Lion and the Unicorn*, London 1941

Polanyi, K., *Origins of Our Times: the great transformation*, London 1945

Plant, R., *Citizens and Rights*, Fabian Society pamphlet, London 1988

Rawls, J., *A Theory of Justice*, Harvard 1972

——, 'Justice as fairness: political not metaphysical', *Philosophy and Public Affairs*, 1985

Runciman, W.G., *Relative Deprivation and Social Welfare*, London 1970

Ryan, A., *Property and Political Theory*, Oxford 1984

——, 'Liberty and Socialism' in *Fabian Essays in Socialist Thought*, ed. B. Pimlott, London 1984

Sandel, M., *Liberalism and the Limits of Justice*, Cambridge 1982

Sen, A., 'The impossibility of a Paretian liberal', *Journal of Political Economy* 78, 1970

——, *Choice, Welfare and Measurement*, Oxford 1982

Schumpeter, J.A., *Capitalism, Socialism and Democracy*, 2nd ed., London 1942

Scott, J., *Capitalist Property and Financial Power*, Brighton 1986

Smith, M., *The Consumer Case for Socialism*, Fabian Society Pamphlet no. 513, London 1986

Strange, S., *Casino Capitalism*, Oxford 1986

Sutcliffe, B., see Green & Sutcliffe

Tocquville, A. de, *De la democratie en Amerique*, Paris 1835-40

Vickers, J., & Yarrow, G., *Privatization: an economic analysis*, Cambridge, Mass. 1988

Weber, M., *From Max Weber: essays in sociology*, translated and edited by Gerth & Mills, New York 1946

——, *The Protestant Ethic and the Spirit of Capitalism*, translated by Parsons, New York 1958

——, *The Methodology of the Social Sciences*, translated and edited by Shils & Finch, New York 1949

Weiss, L., *Creating Capitalism: the state and small business since 1945*, Oxford 1988

Wiggins, D., *Needs, Values, Truth: essays in the philosophy of value*, Oxford 1987

Williams, B., *Ethics and the Limits of Philosophy*, London 1986

Wittgenstein, L., *On Certainty*, Oxford 1969

Wood, A., *Karl Marx*, London 1981

Yarrow, G., see Vickers & Yarrow

Index